Contents

INTRODUCTION

RECIPES

Weeknight Meal Solutions

Prepare healthy meals for family and friends with minimal time and effort using these delicious recipes and tips from Weight Watchers® books.

1 Make meal plans at the beginning of the week.

- Set aside a convenient time each week to plan your meals and make your grocery list.
- Plan your menus around your schedule and the nights when you'll have time to cook.
- Involve your family in meal planning and ask for their help with cooking and cleanup.

2 Stock your pantry and shop less.

- Use the **On-Hand Pantry List** located on the inside front cover of this book to stock your pantry, refrigerator, and freezer. With these items, you'll be able to prepare over one-third of the recipes in this book, including some of our favorite recipes: **Olive and Rosemary Pizza** (page 56), **Fish Tacos** (page 26), and **Easy Veggie Lasagna** (page 31).
- Use canned, prepackaged refrigerated, and frozen fruits and vegetables—they're just as nutritious as fresh.
- If you'd like to use fresh produce, buy it prewashed and already sliced or chopped.
- Organize your pantry so you can easily find the items you need. Keep a list of items you use up so you'll know what needs to be replaced.

3 Streamline your prep and cook times.

- Cook in large batches. Prepare **Versatile Baked Chicken Breast** (page 20) and freeze it in small portions so you'll always have cooked chicken available for quick meals. Cooking your own chicken is healthier and more economical than buying rotisserie or prepackaged cooked chicken at the supermarket.

- Have more than one set of dry and liquid measuring cups and measuring spoons. Rinse, chop, and measure ingredients needed to make the dish before you begin cooking.

4 Cook dishes that yield more than one meal.

- Use today's meals as the basis for tomorrow's lunch or dinner. Prepare **Peach-Glazed Pork Tenderloin** (page 67). Serve one tenderloin the first night and use the second tenderloin to make **Barbecue Pork Baked Potatoes** (page 69) or **Sweet-and-Sour Pork Lo Mein** (page 68) on a different night. Choose simple side dishes with large yields, such as **Broccoli Salad** (page 155), **Buttermilk-Chive Mashed Potatoes** (page 162), **Pesto-Vegetable Medley** (page 164), and **Curried Couscous** (page 170).

5 Make family-friendly recipes healthy.

- Use low-fat dairy products, salad dressings, mayonnaise, and other condiments.
- Use low-fat cooking methods, such as broiling, oven-frying, grilling, and steaming.
- Serve lean cuts of meat, such as skinless chicken breasts and thighs, fish and shellfish, ground round or ground sirloin, flank steak, and pork loin. Include soy products, such as tofu and meatless burger crumbles, in your meals.
- Make healthy versions of kid-friendly entrées, such as **Cornmeal-Crusted Chicken Fingers** (page 88), **Fish Nuggets with Dijon Rémoulade** (page 28), **Skillet Lasagna** (page 138), **"Skinny" Sloppy Joes** (page 49), and **Beefy Chili** (page 141).

10 Fast Fit Facts

from Weight Watchers *Magazine*

1. Cut calories by adding ice cubes made from fruit juice to a glass of water instead of drinking straight juice.

2. Downsize the dish! Serve your ice cream in a teacup instead of a bowl so your portion seems bigger.

3. Burn an extra 100 calories a day by incorporating just an hour of walking, broken into small increments of time, into your workday.

4. If you work at home, pack your lunch and snacks every morning as if you were heading off to work and keep them in the fridge. Take them out at preplanned meal and snack times to prevent grazing.

5. Shop the perimeter of your supermarket, where fresh produce, fish, and meats are displayed. Avoid the snack aisles in the center.

6. Hit the dance floor at your office party. You'll burn 200 calories in half an hour of dancing instead of eating or drinking (based on a 150-pound person).

7. Schedule your walks or workout times on your calendar in red ink. You'll be less tempted to skip them when you treat them as real appointments.

8. When you're eating out at a Mexican restaurant, use a large margarita glass to measure a portion of tortilla chips. One serving of 12 chips (1 ounce) has a ***POINTS***® value of 3.

9. Write down the top 10 reasons you want to lose weight. When your motivation falters, reread your Top 10 list to get back on track.

10. Don't be fooled by smoothies. While they might sound like a healthful snack, they can pack as many calories as a whole meal.

About the Recipes

Weight Watchers® Easy Weeknight Favorites gives you the nutrition facts you need to stay on track.

Each recipe has a complete list of nutrients—including calories, fat, saturated fat, protein, carbohydrates, dietary fiber, cholesterol, iron, sodium, and calcium—as well as a serving size and the yield. This information makes it easy for you to use the recipes in any weight-loss program that you may choose to follow. Measurements are abbreviated g (grams) and mg (milligrams). Nutritional values used in our calculations either come from The Food Processor, Version 7.5 (ESHA Research), or are provided by food manufacturers. Numbers are based on these assumptions:

- Unless otherwise indicated in the ingredient list, servings of meat, poultry, and fish always refer to skinned, boned, and cooked servings.
- When we give a range for an ingredient (3 to 3½ cups flour, for instance), we calculate using the lesser amount.
- Some alcohol calories evaporate during heating; the analysis reflects this.
- Only the amount of marinade absorbed by the food is used in calculations.
- Garnishes and optional ingredients are not included in an analysis.

Safety Note: Cooking spray should never be used near direct heat. Always remove the pan from heat before spraying it with cooking spray.

A Note on Diabetic Exchanges: You may notice that the nutrient analysis for each recipe does not include Diabetic Exchanges. Most dietitians and diabetes educators are now teaching people with diabetes to count total carbohydrates at each meal and snack, rather than counting exchanges. Counting carbohydrates gives people with diabetes more flexibility in their food choices and seems to be an effective way of managing blood glucose.

Almost all of our recipes can be included as part of a diabetic diet by using the carbohydrate amount in the nutrient analysis and incorporating that into the carbohydrate amount recommended by your physician.

POINTS® values and Core Plan® recipes

POINTS values and the Core Plan icon ✓ are part of the flexible food plans offered by Weight Watchers.

POINTS values are part of the Flex Plan, in which every food has a ***POINTS*** value based on calories, fat grams, fiber grams, and portion size. Weight Watchers members on the Flex Plan keep track of ***POINTS*** values to maintain their daily ***POINTS*** Target, while enjoying a full range of food options.

The no-counting Core Plan is based on a list of wholesome, nutritious foods from all food groups—fruits and vegetables; grains and starches; lean meats, fish, and poultry; eggs; and dairy products.

Every recipe in this book includes a ***POINTS*** value. We use a ✓ to identify recipes that fall within the Core Plan. For more information on Weight Watchers, see page 4.

No-Cook Recipes

prep: 12 minutes

Chef's Salad with Creamy Dijon Dressing

Drizzle our zesty homemade dressing over romaine lettuce topped with ham, chicken, eggs, and cheese for a hearty weeknight meal. Since the versatile dressing can easily be doubled, make extra to keep on hand to serve over a side salad later in the week. One tablespoon has a *POINTS* value of 1.

***POINTS* value: 5**

per serving:
CALORIES 212
FAT 8.5g (saturated fat 2.7g)
PROTEIN 27.2g
CARBOHYDRATE 5.1g
FIBER 1.7g
CHOLESTEROL 128mg
IRON 1.8mg
SODIUM 352mg
CALCIUM 100mg

TIP: Save time by cooking the eggs in the microwave. Break each egg into a custard cup; gently prick yolks with tip of a knife or a wooden pick. Cover and microwave at MEDIUM 1 to 1½ minutes or until yolks are firm. Cool completely before chopping.

- 3 cups chopped cooked chicken breast
- 1 (10-ounce) package torn hearts of romaine lettuce
- 2 cups grape tomatoes
- 1 cup diced ham
- ½ cup (2 ounces) reduced-fat shredded sharp Cheddar cheese
- ½ cup sliced ripe olives
- 2 hard-cooked eggs, chopped
- 2 tablespoons light mayonnaise
- 2 tablespoons Dijon mustard
- 1½ teaspoons cider vinegar
- 1 teaspoon sugar
- 1 teaspoon bottled minced garlic
- ⅛ teaspoon salt
- ⅛ teaspoon black pepper

1. Combine first 7 ingredients in a large bowl.

2. Stir together mayonnaise and next 6 ingredients until blended. Add dressing to chicken mixture; toss gently to coat. Serve immediately. Yield: 7 servings (serving size: 2 cups).

prep: 10 minutes

Asian Chicken Salad

The crunchy Napa cabbage and the low-fat sesame-ginger dressing put an Asian-inspired spin on everyday chicken salad. To save time, shred the whole head of Napa cabbage, and then measure what you need for the salad. Store the remaining cabbage in a zip-top bag in the refrigerator for up to two days. Toss it with your favorite low-fat salad dressing for a quick coleslaw.

- 1 small head Napa (Chinese) cabbage, shredded (about 4 cups)
- 1½ cups chopped cooked chicken breast
- 1 cup refrigerated shelled cooked edamame (green soybeans)
- 1 cup chopped English cucumber
- 1 cup matchstick-cut carrots
- ¼ cup thinly sliced green onions (about 1)
- ¼ cup chopped fresh cilantro
- ¼ cup thinly sliced radishes (about 2)
- 5 tablespoons low-fat sesame-ginger dressing (such as Newman's Own)
- 1 (11-ounce) can mandarin oranges, drained
- 5 tablespoons rice noodles (such as La Choy)

1. Combine first 9 ingredients in a large bowl, tossing well. Add oranges, and toss gently.

2. Divide salad mixture among plates. Sprinkle each with rice noodles. Yield: 5 servings (serving size: 2 cups salad and 1 tablespoon noodles).

***POINTS* value: 3**

per serving:
CALORIES 184
FAT 3.9g (saturated fat 0.6g)
PROTEIN 18.7g
CARBOHYDRATE 18g
FIBER 2.7g
CHOLESTEROL 36mg
IRON 1.4mg
SODIUM 328mg
CALCIUM 107mg

TIP: Edamame (green soybeans) are quickly becoming a staple ingredient in many supermarkets. Look for refrigerated shelled cooked edamame in plastic containers in the produce section. Or keep bagged frozen uncooked beans in your freezer. They take about 5 minutes to cook, and leftovers are a filling snack.

prep: 18 minutes

Tex-Mex Layered Salad

Layer the ingredients for the salad and blend the dressing before you leave for work. Pack them in separate containers, and refrigerate. When you get home, toss together the salad and dressing. Serve with multigrain chips or baked tortilla chips to add some crunch.

***POINTS* value: 4**

per serving:
CALORIES 191
FAT 6.1g (saturated fat 2.6g)
PROTEIN 18.2g
CARBOHYDRATE 18.3g
FIBER 3.7g
CHOLESTEROL 41mg
IRON 1.9mg
SODIUM 852mg
CALCIUM 192mg

TIP: If you don't plan to serve this salad all at once, store the salad and the dressing separately in the refrigerator. Right before serving, toss each 1½-cup serving with ¼ cup dressing.

- 2 hearts of romaine lettuce, shredded (about 8½ cups)
- 2 (6-ounce) packages refrigerated grilled chicken breast strips
- 1 (15-ounce) can black beans, rinsed and drained
- 1 (8.75-ounce) can whole-kernel corn, rinsed and drained
- 1 (2-ounce) jar diced pimiento, drained
- 1 cup (4 ounces) shredded 50% reduced-fat Cheddar cheese with jalapeño peppers
- 2 (2.25-ounce) cans sliced ripe olives, drained
- 1 (10-ounce) can diced tomatoes and green chiles, drained
- 1 (8-ounce) carton fat-free sour cream
- ⅓ cup tub-style light cream cheese
- ⅓ cup chopped green onions (about 2)
- 1 teaspoon ground cumin
- 1 garlic clove

1. Layer first 7 ingredients in a large bowl. Cover and chill until ready to serve.

2. Place tomatoes and next 5 ingredients in a blender or food processor; process until smooth. Toss dressing with salad just before serving. Yield: 8 servings (serving size: 1½ cups).

prep: 8 minutes

Roast Beef with Fruit and Mixed Greens ☑

This simple throw-together salad is chock-full of fresh fruit and is a good source of disease-fighting phytochemicals, which can help reduce the risk of heart disease, diabetes, and some cancers.

1 (10-ounce) bag mixed salad greens
2 medium peaches, halved, pitted, and thinly sliced
1 cup blueberries
1 cup seedless red grapes, halved
3/4 pound low-sodium deli roast beef (such as Boar's Head), cubed
1/2 cup fat-free balsamic vinaigrette

1. Combine first 5 ingredients in a large bowl. Drizzle with vinaigrette; toss gently to coat. Serve immediately. Yield: 4 servings (serving size: 3 cups).

***POINTS* value: 4**

per serving:
CALORIES 237
FAT 4.2g (saturated fat 1.6g)
PROTEIN 24.9g
CARBOHYDRATE 28g
FIBER 3.6g
CHOLESTEROL 46mg
IRON 3.5mg
SODIUM 541mg
CALCIUM 45mg

TIP: Leftover chicken, pork loin, or ham may be substituted for the roast beef. Ask someone at your grocer's deli to cut one thick slice of roast beef that weighs 3/4 pound instead of cutting the meat into the usual thin slices. Cube the meat when you get home.

prep: 15 minutes

White Bean and Artichoke Salad

Enjoy this salad as a high-fiber meatless one-dish meal, or add 1 cup of chopped cooked chicken breast for heartier fare with a *POINTS* value of 6 per serving.

***POINTS* value: 4**

per serving:
CALORIES 272
FAT 5g (saturated fat 0.4g)
PROTEIN 11.6g
CARBOHYDRATE 46g
FIBER 10.2g
CHOLESTEROL 0mg
IRON 4.6mg
SODIUM 602mg
CALCIUM 86mg

TIP: Convenience products like canned beans are ideal ingredients to use for no-cook meals, but they're often high in sodium. If you are watching your sodium intake, rinse and drain regular canned beans to decrease the amount of sodium by 40%. Also, look for no-salt-added or reduced-sodium canned products to use instead.

- 2 tablespoons red wine vinegar
- 1/4 teaspoon grated fresh lemon rind
- 2 tablespoons fresh lemon juice
- 1 1/2 teaspoons olive oil
- 1/2 teaspoon honey
- 1/4 teaspoon crushed red pepper
- 1/4 teaspoon salt
- 1/4 teaspoon freshly ground black pepper
- 2 garlic cloves, minced
- 1 red bell pepper, chopped
- 1/2 cup chopped red onion
- 1 (19-ounce) can cannellini beans, rinsed and drained
- 1 (16-ounce) can chickpeas (garbanzo beans), rinsed and drained
- 1 (14-ounce) can quartered artichoke hearts, rinsed, drained, and coarsely chopped
- 1 teaspoon chopped fresh thyme

1. Combine first 9 ingredients in a small bowl. Stir well with a whisk, and set aside.

2. Combine bell pepper and next 5 ingredients in a large bowl, and toss well.

3. Pour dressing over bean mixture, and toss well. Cover and chill until ready to serve. Yield: 3 servings (serving size: 2 cups).

prep: 12 minutes

Turkey and Roasted Red Pepper–Cream Cheese Sandwiches

Dress up ordinary turkey sandwiches with this flavorful and creamy spread. Serve any leftover spread with raw veggies or crackers as a satisfying snack.

½ cup Roasted Red Pepper–Cream Cheese Spread
8 slices double-fiber 100% whole wheat bread (such as Arnold)
8 ounces deli roasted turkey (such as Boar's Head)
1 cup spinach leaves
8 (⅛-inch-thick) slices tomato

1. Spread 1 tablespoon Roasted Red Pepper–Cream Cheese Spread on each slice of bread.

2. Top each of 4 bread slices with 2 ounces turkey, ¼ cup spinach, and 2 slices tomato. Cover with remaining 4 bread slices. Yield: 4 servings (serving size: 1 sandwich).

***POINTS* value: 7**

per serving:
CALORIES 335
FAT 8.5g (saturated fat 2.9g)
PROTEIN 23.8g
CARBOHYDRATE 43.1g
FIBER 10.8g
CHOLESTEROL 40mg
IRON 3.6mg
SODIUM 933mg
CALCIUM 310mg

prep: 8 minutes

Roasted Red Pepper–Cream Cheese Spread

1 (7.25-ounce) jar roasted red bell peppers, drained and finely chopped
1 (8-ounce) tub garden vegetable light cream cheese
1 tablespoon minced fresh basil
½ teaspoon minced garlic
¼ teaspoon freshly ground black pepper

1. Place finely chopped bell pepper on several layers of heavy-duty paper towels; squeeze liquid from bell peppers until barely moist. Place in a small bowl; add remaining ingredients, and stir until blended. Store in refrigerator. Yield: 1⅓ cups (serving size: 1 tablespoon).

***POINTS* value: 1**

per serving:
CALORIES 32
FAT 2.2g (saturated fat 1.5g)
PROTEIN 1g
CARBOHYDRATE 1.4g
FIBER 0g
CHOLESTEROL 10mg
IRON 0mg
SODIUM 106mg
CALCIUM 49mg

prep: 8 minutes

Mediterranean Tuna Salad Pitas

pictured on page 41

We've put a Mediterranean twist on tuna salad, which traditionally calls for copious amounts of mayonnaise. Instead, we used olive oil for richness and added capers, olives, and roasted red bell pepper for salty flavor and color.

***POINTS* value: 7**

per serving:
CALORIES 354
FAT 8.4g (saturated fat 0.9g)
PROTEIN 32.5g
CARBOHYDRATE 39.4g
FIBER 3.5g
CHOLESTEROL 38mg
IRON 2.9mg
SODIUM 872mg
CALCIUM 63mg

TIP: Round out your meal by serving fresh cantaloupe or honeydew melon as a quick and refreshing dessert. One cup of melon has a ***POINTS*** value of 1.

2 (6-ounce) cans albacore tuna in water (such as Bumble Bee Prime Fillet), drained and flaked
½ cup bottled roasted red bell peppers, finely chopped
½ (14-ounce) can quartered artichoke hearts, rinsed, drained, and finely chopped
¼ cup finely chopped flat-leaf parsley
¼ cup chopped pitted kalamata olives
2 tablespoons capers
1 tablespoon extravirgin olive oil
1 tablespoon fresh lemon juice
½ teaspoon freshly ground black pepper
¼ teaspoon salt
4 (6-inch) pitas, cut in half
4 curly leaf lettuce leaves, torn in half

1. Combine first 10 ingredients in a medium bowl, stirring well.

2. Line each pita half with a lettuce leaf. Fill each pita half with about ½ cup tuna salad. Yield: 4 servings (serving size: 2 pita halves).

prep: 12 minutes

Shrimp-Stuffed Pitas

This sensational no-cook meal pairs the refreshing combination of basil, yellow bell pepper, and tomatoes with the delicate flavor of shrimp. We stuffed the shrimp mixture into pita halves, but you can roll up the shrimp mixture in the lettuce leaves to create handheld salads for a *POINTS* value of 4.

- 1 pound medium cooked shrimp, peeled and deveined
- 2 medium tomatoes, seeded and chopped
- 1 finely chopped yellow bell pepper
- ⅓ cup minced onion
- ¼ cup light mayonnaise
- ¼ cup chopped fresh basil
- 2 teaspoons lemon juice
- ¼ teaspoon salt
- ¼ teaspoon black pepper
- 4 (6-inch) whole wheat pitas, cut in half
- 4 curly leaf lettuce leaves, torn in half

1. Combine first 9 ingredients in a medium bowl; toss well.

2. Line each pita half with a lettuce leaf. Fill each pita half with ½ cup shrimp salad using a slotted spoon. Serve immediately. Yield: 4 servings (serving size: 2 pita halves).

***POINTS* value: 6**

per serving:
CALORIES 332
FAT 6.4g (saturated fat 1.1g)
PROTEIN 31.1g
CARBOHYDRATE 39g
FIBER 4.6g
CHOLESTEROL 226mg
IRON 5.9mg
SODIUM 654mg
CALCIUM 106mg

TIP: It's important to seed the tomatoes for this salad to keep the mixture from being too wet. To seed a tomato quickly, cut it in half crosswise. Use a knife, a small spoon, or your finger to push out the seeds. Or lightly squeeze each half, and the seeds will slip out.

prep: 13 minutes

Shrimp Spring Rolls

These flavorful spring rolls are packed with shrimp and fresh veggies. For an extra punch of flavor, serve them with your favorite dipping sauce. We suggest sweet and spicy hoisin sauce or sweet-and-sour plum sauce.

***POINTS* value: 5**

per serving:
CALORIES 233
FAT 8.3g (saturated fat 2g)
PROTEIN 20.4g
CARBOHYDRATE 17.4g
FIBER 2.3g
CHOLESTEROL 148mg
IRON 2.7mg
SODIUM 362mg
CALCIUM 58mg

½ pound large cooked shrimp, peeled and chopped into thirds
¾ cups matchstick-cut carrots
⅓ cup minced green onions
¼ cup cucumber, halved lengthwise and thinly sliced lengthwise
¼ cup chopped dry-roasted peanuts
6 (8½-inch) round rice paper sheets
1 tablespoon hoisin sauce, divided

1. Combine first 5 ingredients in a small bowl; set aside.

2. Add warm water to a large shallow dish to a depth of 1 inch. Place 1 rice paper sheet in water. Let stand about 10 seconds or just until soft.

3. Place softened sheet on a flat surface; spread ½ teaspoon hoisin sauce on bottom half. Arrange ½ cup filling over bottom third of rice paper sheet. Fold bottom of rice paper sheet over filling, pressing slightly. Fold sides of sheet over filling, overlapping in center to form a tight roll. Roll up spring roll, jelly-roll fashion, and gently press seam to seal.

4. Repeat procedure with remaining rice paper sheets, hoisin sauce, and shrimp mixture. Serve immediately, or wrap in plastic wrap and chill up to 1 hour. Yield: 3 servings (serving size: 2 rolls).

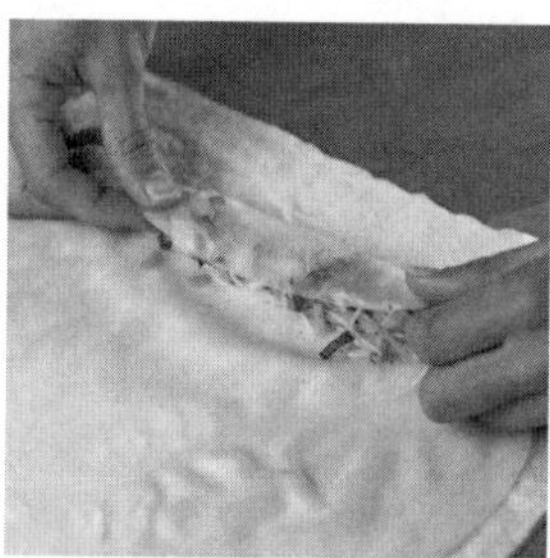

1. Arrange ½ cup filling over bottom third of rice paper sheet. Fold bottom of rice paper sheet over filling, pressing slightly.

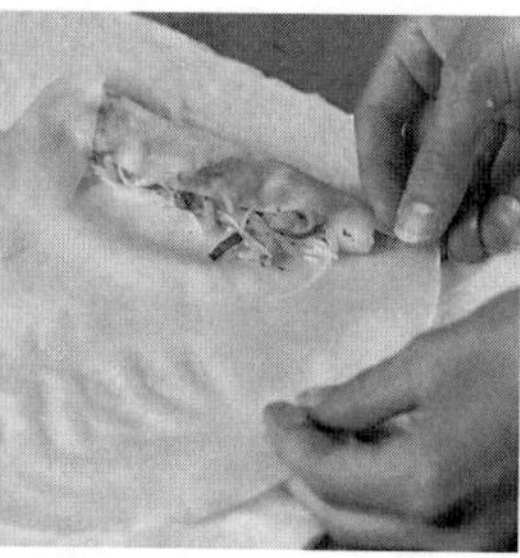

2. Fold sides of sheet over filling, overlapping in center to form a tight roll.

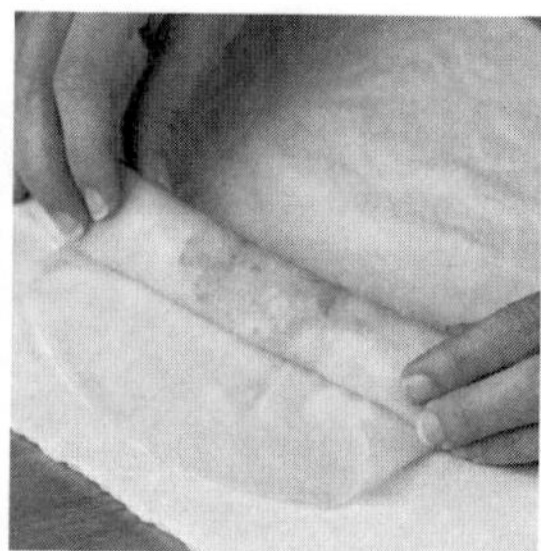

3. Roll up jelly-roll fashion, and gently press seam to seal.

prep: 11 minutes

Roast Beef Wraps

pictured on page 122

Silence the calls of "What's for dinner?" by asking your family to help make these supereasy sandwiches.

- 1 tablespoon red wine vinegar
- 1 teaspoon sugar
- ½ cup thinly sliced red onion
- 2 tablespoons fat-free sour cream
- 2 tablespoons fat-free mayonnaise
- 2 tablespoons crumbled blue cheese
- ¼ teaspoon freshly ground black pepper
- 4 (8-inch) stone-ground whole wheat tortillas (such as Tamxico's)
- ½ pound thinly sliced extralean deli roast beef
- 2 cups arugula or spinach leaves

1. Combine vinegar and sugar in a small bowl; stir until sugar dissolves. Add onion, and toss well. Set aside.

2. Combine sour cream and next 3 ingredients. Spread 1½ tablespoons sour cream mixture over each tortilla. Top evenly with roast beef and arugula. Spoon marinated onions evenly over arugula using a slotted spoon. Roll up wraps tightly; cut each in half crosswise, and secure with a wooden pick, if necessary. Yield: 4 servings (serving size: 2 tortilla halves).

***POINTS* value: 4**

per serving:
CALORIES 209
FAT 5g (saturated fat 1.3g)
PROTEIN 13.9g
CARBOHYDRATE 25.9g
FIBER 3.6g
CHOLESTEROL 25mg
IRON 2mg
SODIUM 778mg
CALCIUM 99mg

TIP: Replace the usual bag of chips with a ½-cup serving of crisp baby carrots for a quick meal with a total ***POINTS*** value of 4.

prep: 20 minutes

Veggie Hummus Wraps

By keeping items such as chickpeas (garbanzo beans), garlic, lemon juice, and olive oil on hand, you'll be able to quickly prepare this homemade version of hummus, which has fewer calories and less fat and salt than store-bought varieties.

***POINTS* value: 5**

per serving:
CALORIES 256
FAT 8.3g (saturated fat 1.6g)
PROTEIN 8.6g
CARBOHYDRATE 37.2g
FIBER 5.3g
CHOLESTEROL 3mg
IRON 0.9mg
SODIUM 849mg
CALCIUM 59mg

TIP: Look for bottled cloves of garlic in the produce section of your supermarket. If you have bottled minced garlic on hand, substitute 2 teaspoons for 2 whole cloves.

1 (15-ounce) can chickpeas (garbanzo beans), rinsed and drained
2 bottled garlic cloves
2 tablespoons fresh lemon juice
1 tablespoon olive oil
¼ teaspoon ground cumin
¼ teaspoon salt
6 (8-inch) flour tortillas
2 cups shredded iceberg lettuce
1½ cups matchstick-cut carrots
1½ cups grape tomatoes, coarsely chopped
½ cup coarsely chopped pitted kalamata olives
½ cup (2 ounces) crumbled reduced-fat feta cheese

1. Place first 6 ingredients in a blender or food processor; process until smooth, scraping sides of bowl once.

2. Warm tortillas according to package directions.

3. Spread ¼ cup hummus over each tortilla. Divide lettuce and next 4 ingredients evenly among tortillas. Fold in bottom of each tortilla, and roll up. Yield: 6 servings (serving size: 1 wrap).

On-Hand Dinners

4 Essential Ingredients for Quick & Easy Meals

Keep cooked chicken, frozen grouper fillets, meatless burger crumbles, or Italian cheese-flavored pizza crust on hand to jump-start healthy weeknight dinners.

Cooked Chicken

Delicious in:

- Hawaiian Chicken Sandwiches (page 22)
- Tomato, Chicken, and Feta Pasta (page 23)
- Southwestern Chicken Soup (page 24)
- Chicken Quesadillas (page 25)
- Southwestern Chicken Pizza (page 52)

Health Benefits:

- Precooked chicken—such as rotisserie, packaged grilled chicken strips, and frozen chopped cooked chicken—is certainly convenient, but it's also five times higher in sodium than chicken you cook yourself. When you have the time, we suggest that you cook your own chicken.

Freezing and Thawing Directions:

- When you precook chicken, make sure to refrigerate it within two hours of cooking. First, allow the chicken to cool; debone, if needed. Chop, shred, or slice the meat, and place it in shallow airtight containers. Store it in the refrigerator for up to two days. Or wrap the cooled meat in heavy-duty plastic wrap or aluminum foil. You may also place it in freezer-safe containers and freeze it for up to four months.
- For the best results, thaw cooked chicken in the refrigerator for 24 hours.
- When you're in a hurry, thaw chicken in the microwave at MEDIUM 8 minutes, stirring after 4 minutes (it should feel cool and pliable).

Versatile Baked Chicken Breast ☑

POINTS value: 4

prep: 30 minutes ∞ **cook:** 25 minutes

5¼ pounds skinless, boneless chicken breast halves (about 16 breast halves)
1 teaspoon black pepper
¾ teaspoon salt

1. Preheat oven to 350°.
2. Divide chicken evenly between 2 ungreased baking sheets. Sprinkle with pepper and salt.
3. Bake at 350° for 25 to 30 minutes or until done
4. Cool completely. After chicken has cooled, divide into portions for the On-Hand Dinner recipes listed above: 5 cups sliced, 5¼ cups chopped, and 1½ cups shredded.
5. Place in freezer-safe containers, and freeze until ready to use. Yield: 14 servings (serving size: about 4 ounces)

per serving: CALORIES 188; FAT 2.1g (saturated fat 0.6g); PROTEIN 39.3g; CARBOHYDRATE 0.1g; FIBER 0g; CHOLESTEROL 99mg; IRON 1.2mg; SODIUM 235mg; CALCIUM 19mg

Frozen Grouper Fillets

Delicious in:

- Fish Tacos (page 26)
- Grilled Fish with Pineapple Salsa (page 27)
- Fish Nuggets with Dijon Rémoulade (page 28)
- Skillet Grouper with Pan-Roasted Tomatoes (page 29)
- Grouper with Lemon-Caper Sauce (page 30)

Health Benefits:

• Fish promotes heart health because it contains omega-3 fatty acids and is lower in saturated fat than other meats.

Purchasing:

• Fish is now being processed and frozen on large fishing boats while the boats are still at sea, which improves the overall quality of the fish and increases the amount and variety of fish available to consumers.

• Look for vacuum-packed frozen fish. Make sure the package has its original shape and the wrapping is intact with no visible ice crystals.

• Frozen seafood can be stored in the freezer for up to six months.

Thawing Directions:

• The best way to thaw a 1-pound package of frozen fish is in the refrigerator; the fish will defrost in 24 hours.

• A quick-thaw method is to place frozen fish in its original wrapper in a sink of cold water or under cold running water. A one-pound package will thaw in about an hour.

• If using the microwave, a pound of fillets will defrost in 5 to 6 minutes on 30% power. Be careful not to overheat the fish because it will begin to cook.

Meatless Burger Crumbles

Delicious in:

- Easy Veggie Lasagna (page 31)
- Hearty Vegetable Soup (page 32)
- "Skinny" Sloppy Joes (page 49)
- Soft Tacos (page 50)
- Veggie Chili (page 51)

Health Benefits:

• Meatless burger crumbles are a healthy alternative to ground beef because they are lower in fat and saturated fat.

Beef/Crumbles	% Fat
Ground Beef	30%
Ground Chuck	20%
Ground Round	11%
Ground Sirloin	7%
Meatless Burger Crumbles	4%

Purchasing:

• Meatless burger crumbles are recipe-ready. Use one 12-ounce package of crumbles for 1 pound of uncooked ground beef.

• You'll find the crumbles in the frozen foods section of the grocery store alongside the other frozen natural or organic foods.

Italian Cheese-Flavored Pizza Crust

Delicious in:

- Southwestern Chicken Pizza (page 52)
- Ham and Tomato Pizza (page 53)
- Polynesian Pizza (page 54)
- Rustic Tomato-Olive Pizza (page 55)
- Olive and Rosemary Pizza (page 56)

Health Benefits:

• Make your own delicious pizza with a lower ***POINTS*** value than delivery pizza. Our pizzas have a ***POINTS*** value of 4 per slice, while a large one-topping pizza has a ***POINTS*** value of 6 to 9 per slice. Use either a 10-ounce thin crust or a 14-ounce regular crust for any of our pizzas. Generally, the 14-ounce crust provides an additional ***POINTS*** value of 1 per slice.

Purchasing:

• Look for Italian cheese-flavored pizza crust in the bread section or on its own display rack at your supermarket.

Freezing and Thawing Directions:

• To freeze a pizza crust, place it in a freezer safe zip-top bag. To thaw, let it stand at room temperature for 10 to 15 minutes.

prep: 5 minutes ∞ **cook:** 12 minutes

Hawaiian Chicken Sandwiches

Perk up the flavor of plain chicken sandwiches by adding caramelized pineapple slices and an herbed mayonnaise.

***POINTS* value: 7**

per serving:
CALORIES 340
FAT 10.6g (saturated fat 3.1g)
PROTEIN 28.9g
CARBOHYDRATE 32.9g
FIBER 3.9g
CHOLESTEROL 66mg
IRON 2mg
SODIUM 519mg
CALCIUM 161mg

TIP: Cooking the pineapple enhances its natural sweetness while giving it a rich golden color. Pay close attention—the pineapple and juices can burn quickly and will turn bitter.

¼ cup light mayonnaise
½ teaspoon dried tarragon
4 (1½-ounce) whole wheat hamburger buns
2 cups frozen sliced **Versatile Baked Chicken Breast** (page 20), thawed
½ cup shredded part-skim mozzarella cheese
1 (8-ounce) can pineapple slices in juice, undrained
Torn hearts of romaine lettuce (optional)

1. Preheat oven to 350°.

2. Combine mayonnaise and tarragon in a small bowl; set aside.

3. Place hamburger buns, cut sides up, on a baking sheet. Arrange chicken evenly over bottom halves of buns, and top with cheese. Bake top and bottom halves of buns at 350° for 5 minutes or until buns are golden and cheese melts.

4. While buns bake, heat a large nonstick skillet over medium-high heat. Remove pineapple slices from can, reserving juice. Pat slices dry with paper towels. Add pineapple slices to hot pan, and cook 3 minutes on each side or until golden brown. Add reserved pineapple juice; cook until liquid evaporates, scraping pan to loosen browned bits. Remove pan from heat.

5. Place pineapple on top of chicken and melted cheese. Top pineapple with romaine lettuce, if desired. Spread tarragon mayonnaise evenly on top halves of buns; place on top of sandwiches. Yield: 4 servings (serving size: 1 sandwich).

prep: 5 minutes ∞ **cook:** 14 minutes

Tomato, Chicken, and Feta Pasta

This superfast pasta dish with olives and feta cheese is delicious served warm, but leftovers are equally good served cold.

- 4 ounces uncooked penne pasta
- 1 teaspoon olive oil
- 1 teaspoon bottled minced garlic
- 1 (14.5-ounce) can diced tomatoes with basil, garlic, and oregano, undrained
- 3 cups frozen chopped **Versatile Baked Chicken Breast** (page 20), thawed
- 1/4 cup sliced pitted kalamata olives
- 1/4 teaspoon freshly ground black pepper
- 6 tablespoons reduced-fat crumbled feta cheese

1. Cook pasta according to package directions, omitting salt and fat.

2. While pasta cooks, heat oil in a nonstick skillet over medium heat; add garlic, and cook 1 minute. Add tomatoes and next 3 ingredients; simmer 6 minutes or until thoroughly heated, stirring occasionally.

3. Combine tomato mixture and pasta; top with feta cheese. Serve immediately. Yield: 6 servings (serving size: 1 cup).

***POINTS* value: 5**

per serving:
CALORIES 225
FAT 5.5g (saturated fat 1.8g)
PROTEIN 22g
CARBOHYDRATE 21.4g
FIBER 1.5g
CHOLESTEROL 43mg
IRON 2.1mg
SODIUM 740mg
CALCIUM 97mg

TIP: Look for pitted kalamata olives in the condiment section at your grocery store. If you can't find pitted olives, place the olives on a cutting board. Lay the wide, flat side of a heavy chef's knife on top of the olives, and give a good, sharp whack to the blade. The olives will pop open, exposing the pits for easy removal.

prep: 8 minutes ∞ **cook:** 23 minutes

Southwestern Chicken Soup

This soup is chock-full of chicken, pinto beans, and corn, making it a satisfying one-dish meal. For a refreshing and simple dessert, serve with 1 cup of fresh orange slices for a meal with a *POINTS* value of 4 per serving.

***POINTS* value: 3**

per serving:
CALORIES 188
FAT 4.8g (saturated fat 1.5g)
PROTEIN 17.2g
CARBOHYDRATE 18.1g
FIBER 4.6g
CHOLESTEROL 37mg
IRON 1.3mg
SODIUM 598mg
CALCIUM 59mg

TIP: There's no reason to thaw the chicken before adding it to the pot. It will thaw as the soup mixture comes to a boil.

1 teaspoon olive oil
½ cup frozen chopped onion
2 teaspoons bottled minced garlic
2¼ cups frozen chopped Versatile Baked Chicken Breast (page 20)
1 (16-ounce) can pinto beans, rinsed and drained
1 (14.5-ounce) can diced tomatoes, undrained
1 (14-ounce) can fat-free, less-sodium chicken broth
1 (8¾-ounce) can whole-kernel corn, undrained
1 (4.5-ounce) can chopped green chiles, undrained
½ teaspoon chili powder
½ teaspoon ground cumin
6 tablespoons reduced-fat sour cream

1. Heat oil in a Dutch oven over medium-high heat. Add onion and garlic; sauté 2 to 3 minutes.

2. Add chicken and next 7 ingredients. Bring to a boil; reduce heat, and simmer 15 minutes. Ladle soup into bowls; top with sour cream. Yield: 6 servings (serving size: 2 cups soup and 1 tablespoon sour cream).

prep: 2 minutes ∞ **cook:** 23 minutes

Chicken Quesadillas

pictured on page 127

Use Versatile Baked Chicken Breast to make a healthy version of chicken quesadillas. Reduced-fat cheese and sour cream create a restaurant-quality dish with a *POINTS* value of 7.

- 1 teaspoon olive oil
- 1 teaspoon bottled minced garlic
- 3 cups frozen sliced Versatile Baked Chicken Breast (page 20), thawed
- 1 (16-ounce) package frozen bell pepper and onion stir-fry, thawed
- 2 teaspoons salt-free Southwest chipotle seasoning (such as Mrs. Dash)
- 1/8 teaspoon salt
- 1 (4.5-ounce) can chopped green chiles, drained
- Cooking spray
- 6 (8-inch) flour tortillas
- 1 1/2 cups preshredded reduced-fat Mexican blend cheese or reduced-fat shredded sharp Cheddar cheese
- 3/4 cup refrigerated fresh salsa
- Reduced-fat sour cream (optional)

1. Heat oil in a large nonstick skillet over medium-high heat. Add garlic, and sauté 1 minute. Add chicken and next 4 ingredients; sauté 4 to 6 minutes or until chicken and vegetables are thoroughly heated. Remove chicken mixture from pan; cover and keep warm.

2. Wipe pan dry with a paper towel. Coat pan with cooking spray, and place over medium-high heat. Place 2 tortillas in pan. Place about 1 cup chicken mixture and 1/4 cup cheese on 1 side of each tortilla; fold in half. Cook 3 minutes on each side or until golden brown. Repeat procedure with remaining tortillas, chicken mixture, and cheese. Cut each quesadilla into 2 wedges, and top with salsa. Serve with sour cream, if desired. Yield: 6 servings (serving size: 2 quesadilla wedges and 2 tablespoons salsa).

***POINTS* value: 7**

per serving:
CALORIES 336
FAT 8.7g (saturated fat 4.4g)
PROTEIN 31.3g
CARBOHYDRATE 30.7g
FIBER 2g
CHOLESTEROL 69mg
IRON 0.8mg
SODIUM 793mg
CALCIUM 264mg

TIP: Thaw the bell pepper and onion stir-fry in the microwave at MEDIUM 5 minutes; drain excess liquid.

prep: 8 minutes ∞ **cook:** 10 minutes

Fish Tacos

Freshly squeezed lime juice is the secret ingredient in these fish tacos. It adds a refreshing tartness to the chunks of fish and intensifies the tangy flavor of the sour cream topping.

***POINTS* value: 4**

per serving:
CALORIES 213
FAT 4.6g (saturated fat 1g)
PROTEIN 20.2g
CARBOHYDRATE 21.8g
FIBER 1.2g
CHOLESTEROL 35mg
IRON 0.9mg
SODIUM 444mg
CALCIUM 38mg

TIP: One medium lime yields about 1½ tablespoons of juice. You'll get more juice out of a lime if you bring it to room temperature before squeezing the juice.

¼ cup reduced-fat sour cream
2 tablespoons fresh lime juice
½ teaspoon ground cumin
¼ teaspoon chili powder
1 teaspoon salt-free Southwest chipotle seasoning (such as Mrs. Dash)
¼ teaspoon salt
4 (6-ounce) **frozen grouper fillets**, thawed
¼ cup all-purpose flour
1 tablespoon olive oil
2 lime wedges
8 (6-inch) flour tortillas
1 cup shredded iceberg lettuce
½ cup refrigerated fresh salsa

1. Combine first 4 ingredients in a small bowl; set aside.

2. Sprinkle seasoning and salt on fish; dredge fish in flour. Heat oil in a large nonstick skillet over medium-high heat. Add fish; cook 4 minutes on each side or until fish flakes easily when tested with a fork. Remove from pan, and squeeze lime wedges over fish. Separate fish into chunks using a fork.

3. Heat tortillas according to package directions. Top each tortilla with ½ cup fish. Divide lettuce and salsa evenly among tacos, and top evenly with sour cream mixture. Yield: 8 servings (serving size: 1 taco).

prep: 2 minutes ∞ **cook:** 8 minutes

Grilled Fish with Pineapple Salsa

We tasted the fish first with regular refrigerated salsa, but we wanted a bit of a sweet taste to complete the dish. Stirring pineapple tidbits into the salsa was a quick and delicious solution.

- ½ cup refrigerated fresh salsa
- 1 (8-ounce) can pineapple tidbits, drained
- 4 (6-ounce) **frozen grouper fillets**, thawed
- Olive oil–flavored cooking spray
- 1 teaspoon bottled minced garlic
- ½ teaspoon salt
- ¼ teaspoon freshly ground black pepper
- Chopped fresh cilantro (optional)

1. Prepare grill.

2. Combine salsa and pineapple; set aside.

3. Coat fish with cooking spray, and rub garlic evenly over fish. Sprinkle fish evenly with salt and pepper. Place fish on grill rack coated with cooking spray. Cover and grill 4 to 5 minutes on each side or until fish flakes easily when tested with a fork. Serve fish with pineapple salsa; sprinkle with chopped fresh cilantro, if desired. Yield: 4 servings (serving size: 1 grouper fillet and ¼ cup salsa).

***POINTS* value: 4**

per serving:
CALORIES 197
FAT 1.9g (saturated fat 0.4g)
PROTEIN 33g
CARBOHYDRATE 7.9g
FIBER 0.5g
CHOLESTEROL 63mg
IRON 1.7mg
SODIUM 460mg
CALCIUM 47mg

TIP: We recommend cleaning your grill twice: once after preheating the grill, and again when you've finished grilling. Use a metal spatula and a wire brush to scrape the grates clean.

prep: 9 minutes ∞ **cook:** 10 minutes

Fish Nuggets with Dijon Rémoulade

These big chunks of lean grouper are dusted with cornmeal and then oven-fried. Compared to store-bought or fast-food fish sticks, our light, crunchy coating doesn't overpower the delicate flavor and texture of the fish.

***POINTS* value: 7**

per serving:
CALORIES 314
FAT 15.5g (saturated fat 2.4g)
PROTEIN 33.7g
CARBOHYDRATE 8.5g
FIBER 0.7g
CHOLESTEROL 70mg
IRON 1.8mg
SODIUM 709mg
CALCIUM 49mg

TIP: The fish will cook faster and more evenly if you don't crowd it in the skillet. Instead, cook it in two batches.

- 1 tablespoon capers, drained
- 1/3 cup light mayonnaise
- 2 tablespoons creamy mustard blend (such as Dijonnaise)
- 4 (6-ounce) **frozen grouper fillets**, thawed and cut crosswise into 4 (1-inch) pieces
- 1/2 teaspoon salt
- 1/2 teaspoon freshly ground black pepper
- 3 tablespoons yellow cornmeal
- 2 tablespoons olive oil

1. Place capers in a small bowl; mash with a fork. Add mayonnaise and mustard blend to capers; stir until well blended. Set aside.

2. Sprinkle fish with salt and pepper. Dredge in cornmeal.

3. Heat 1 tablespoon oil in a large nonstick skillet over medium-high heat. Add half of fish; cook 2 to 3 minutes on each side or until fish flakes easily when tested with a fork. Repeat with remaining oil and fish. Serve with rémoulade. Yield: 4 servings (serving size: 4 grouper pieces and 2 tablespoons rémoulade).

prep: 6 minutes ◦◦ **cook:** 21 minutes

Skillet Grouper with Pan-Roasted Tomatoes

pictured on page 45

Pan-roasting the tomatoes, garlic, and olives is a quick way to intensify their flavors and create a chunky sauce in which to poach the fish.

- 1 tablespoon olive oil
- 2 pints grape tomatoes
- 8 garlic cloves, crushed
- 1 tablespoon capers
- ¼ cup chopped pitted kalamata olives
- 1 tablespoon balsamic vinegar
- 4 (6-ounce) **frozen grouper fillets**, thawed
- 1 teaspoon Greek seasoning
- ½ teaspoon freshly ground black pepper

1. Heat oil in a large nonstick skillet over medium-high heat. Add tomatoes, garlic, capers, and olives; cook 8 minutes or until tomatoes are lightly browned and bursting open, stirring frequently. Stir in balsamic vinegar.

2. Sprinkle fish evenly with seasoning and pepper. Add fish to pan, nestling fish into tomato mixture. Cover and cook 12 minutes or until fish flakes easily when tested with a fork. Serve immediately. Yield: 4 servings (serving size: 1 grouper fillet and ½ cup tomato mixture).

***POINTS* value: 6**

per serving:
CALORIES 276
FAT 10.3g (saturated fat 1.5g)
PROTEIN 35g
CARBOHYDRATE 10.3g
FIBER 2.2g
CHOLESTEROL 63mg
IRON 2.2mg
SODIUM 693mg
CALCIUM 80mg

TIP: Using a garlic press is the easiest and most efficient method of crushing garlic for recipes. You'll be able to get both the garlic and its juice.

prep: 4 minutes ∞ **cook:** 10 minutes

Grouper with Lemon-Caper Sauce

Traditionally, a pat of butter is added near the end of the cook time to thicken the lemon-caper sauce, but we've discovered that a little cornstarch will thicken the sause without adding fat.

***POINTS* value: 4**

per serving:
CALORIES 185
FAT 4.1g (saturated fat 0.7g)
PROTEIN 33.1g
CARBOHYDRATE 2.6g
FIBER 0.2g
CHOLESTEROL 63mg
IRON 1.6mg
SODIUM 424mg
CALCIUM 49mg

TIP: You'll find capers in the condiment section of your supermarket. Look for the smaller immature buds. They're a little more expensive, but they're also more intensely flavored and will last up to a year in the refrigerator.

3 tablespoons water, divided
1 teaspoon cornstarch
4 (6-ounce) **frozen grouper fillets**, thawed
½ teaspoon salt, divided
½ teaspoon fresh ground black pepper, divided
2 teaspoons olive oil
¼ teaspoon grated fresh lemon rind
⅓ cup fresh lemon juice
2 teaspoons capers

1. Combine 1 tablespoon water and cornstarch in a small bowl, stirring with a whisk. Set aside.

2. Sprinkle fish on both sides with ¼ teaspoon salt and ¼ teaspoon pepper.

3. Heat oil in a large nonstick skillet over medium-high heat. Add fish, and cook 3 to 4 minutes on each side or until fish flakes easily with a fork. Remove from pan, and keep warm.

4. Add remaining 2 tablespoons water, remaining ¼ teaspoon each of salt and pepper, lemon rind, lemon juice, and capers to pan; cook 2 minutes. Remove from heat, and stir in cornstarch mixture; cook 1 minute or until thick. Serve sauce over fish. Yield: 4 servings (serving size: 1 grouper fillet and 1 tablespoon sauce).

prep: 11 minutes ∞ **cook:** 1 hour and 3 minutes ∞ **other:** 10 minutes

Easy Veggie Lasagna

This cheesy vegetarian lasagna can be quickly assembled to create a satisfying meatless one-dish meal that's perfect for any busy weeknight menu.

- 9 uncooked lasagna noodles
- Cooking spray
- 1 tablespoon olive oil
- ½ cup frozen chopped onion
- 1 (16-ounce) package frozen bell pepper and onion stir-fry
- ½ (10-ounce) package matchstick-cut carrots
- ½ teaspoon dried oregano
- ¼ teaspoon black pepper
- 1 teaspoon bottled minced garlic
- ½ cup chopped pitted kalamata olives
- 2 cups frozen **meatless burger crumbles** (such as Morningstar Farms)
- 1 (26-ounce) jar tomato-basil pasta sauce (such as Classico)
- 1 (15-ounce) container part-skim ricotta cheese
- 2½ cups shredded part-skim mozzarella cheese or shredded mozzarella and Asiago with roasted garlic cheese blend (such as Sargento)

1. Preheat oven to 350°.

2. Cook lasagna noodles according to package directions, omitting salt and fat. Drain and rinse with cold water. Drain.

3. While noodles cook, coat a 13 x 9–inch baking dish with cooking spray; set aside. Heat oil in a large skillet over medium-high heat. Add onion and next 4 ingredients; cook until vegetables are crisp-tender. Add garlic and olives; cook 2 minutes. Stir in burger crumbles and pasta sauce. Cover; reduce heat to low, and simmer 10 minutes, stirring occasionally.

4. Place 3 noodles in prepared baking dish; top with one-third of pasta sauce mixture, half of ricotta cheese, and one-third of mozzarella cheese. Repeat layers once. Top second layer with remaining 3 noodles and pasta sauce mixture; sprinkle with remaining mozzarella cheese. Cover with foil.

5. Bake at 350° for 30 minutes. Uncover and bake 15 minutes or until cheese is bubbly. Let stand 10 minutes before serving. Cut into 8 equal portions. Yield: 8 servings (serving size: 1 [4½ x 3¼–inch] rectangle).

***POINTS* value: 8**

per serving:
CALORIES 362
FAT 14.2g (saturated fat 6.5g)
PROTEIN 23g
CARBOHYDRATE 37.5g
FIBER 4.2g
CHOLESTEROL 42mg
IRON 2.5mg
SODIUM 796mg
CALCIUM 406mg

TIP: Look for bags of meatless burger crumbles in the frozen food section of your supermarket alongside other frozen vegetarian foods.

prep: 3 minutes ∞ **cook:** 38 minutes

Hearty Vegetable Soup

Keep your pantry and freezer stocked with the ingredients for this soup and you'll always be prepared for a quick meal. There's very little measuring required, and because you only use one pan, cleanup is easy.

***POINTS* value: 3**

per serving:
CALORIES 174
FAT 3.3g (saturated fat 0g)
PROTEIN 12g
CARBOHYDRATE 26.6g
FIBER 6.7g
CHOLESTEROL 0mg
IRON 3mg
SODIUM 845mg
CALCIUM 57mg

TIP: Hot sauce is a fiery condiment that is used to add heat to a variety of dishes. It is usually made from chile peppers, vinegar, and salt.

- 1 (15-ounce) can black beans, rinsed and drained
- 1 (14.5-ounce) can diced tomatoes, undrained
- 1 (4.5-ounce) can chopped green chiles, undrained
- 1 (12-ounce) package frozen **meatless burger crumbles** (such as Morningstar Farms)
- 3¼ cups water
- 1 (14-ounce) can vegetable broth (such as Swanson)
- 1 (16-ounce) package frozen bell pepper and onion stir-fry
- 1 cup frozen chopped onion
- 2 (8¾-ounce) cans whole-kernel corn, drained
- 2 teaspoons bottled minced garlic
- 1 tablespoon ground cumin
- ½ teaspoon dried oregano
- ¼ teaspoon dried thyme
- 1 teaspoon hot sauce

1. Combine all ingredients in a large Dutch oven. Bring to a boil; cover, reduce heat to low, and simmer 30 minutes, stirring occasionally. Yield: 8 servings (serving size: 1½ cups).

Grilled Chicken with Fresh Orange Salsa, page 84

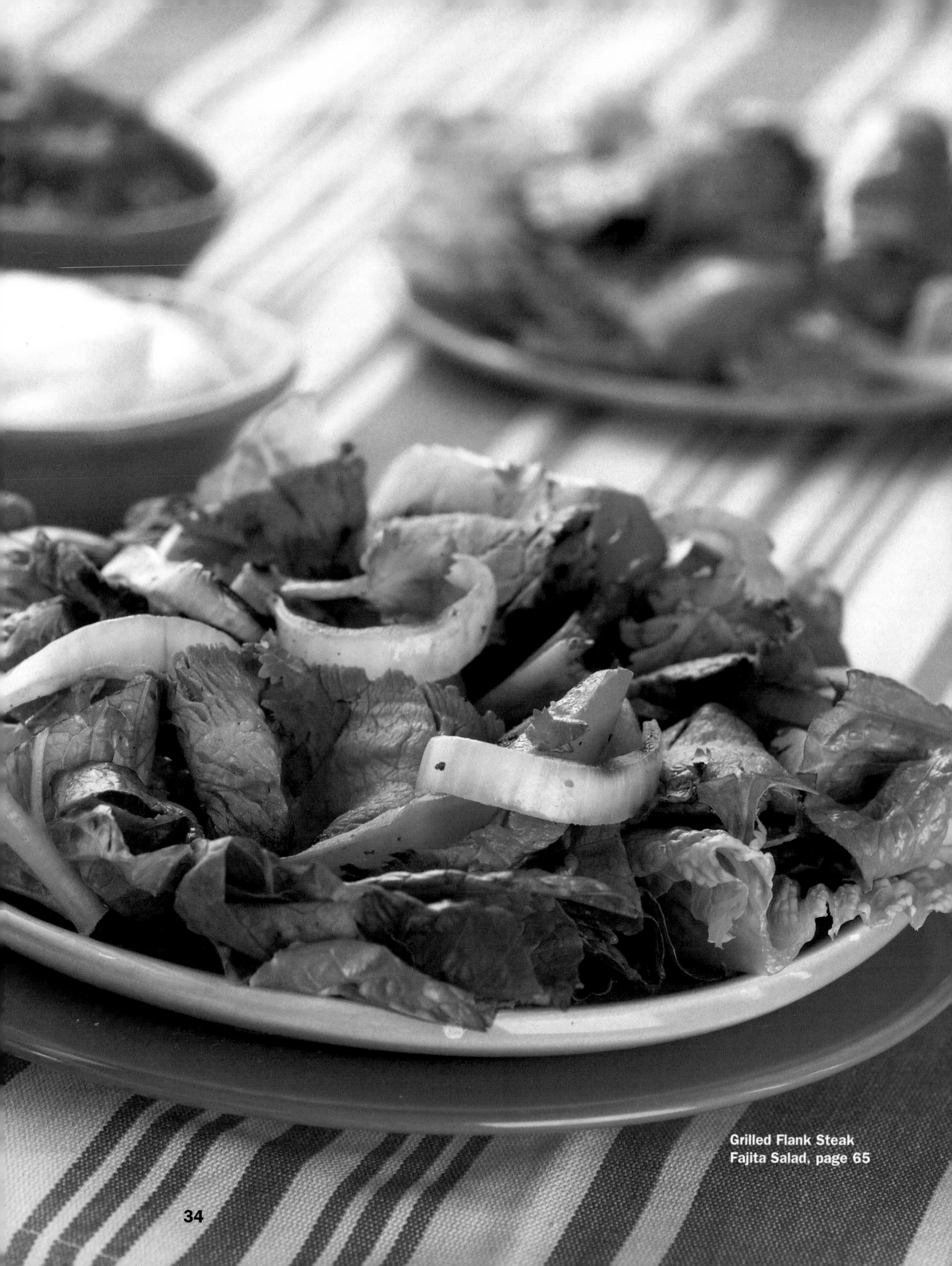

Grilled Flank Steak
Fajita Salad, page 65

Beefy Chili,
page 141

Cucumber and Honeydew Salad, page 156

Seared Chicken Breast with Pan Gravy, page 85

Asian Pepper Steak, page 142

Polenta with Olives, Tomatoes, and Feta, page 151

Braised Steak with Mushrooms and Sour Cream, page 144

Mediterranean Tuna Salad Pitas, page 14

Blueberry-Balsamic Pork Cutlets, page 102

Tortelloni with Grilled Vegetables, page 71

Pulled-Pork Sandwiches, **page 105**

Chocolate Cream Pie, page 186

Pesto-Vegetable Medley, page 164

prep: 4 minutes ∞ **cook:** 9 minutes

"Skinny" Sloppy Joes

Your family will never guess that this hearty knife-and-fork sandwich is a reduced-fat vegetarian version of traditional ground-beef sloppy joes.

- 1 teaspoon olive oil
- ½ cup frozen chopped onion
- 2 cups frozen **meatless burger crumbles** (such as Morningstar Farms)
- 1 (8-ounce) can tomato sauce
- ½ cup ketchup
- 1 tablespoon brown sugar
- 1 tablespoon prepared mustard
- ½ teaspoon dry mustard
- ½ teaspoon bottled minced garlic
- ½ teaspoon fresh lemon juice
- ¼ teaspoon paprika
- ¼ teaspoon black pepper
- 1 teaspoon cider vinegar
- 6 (1½-ounce) whole wheat hamburger buns

1. Heat oil in a large nonstick skillet over medium-high heat. Add onion; cook 3 minutes or until tender. Add burger crumbles and next 9 ingredients; stir well.

2. Cook over medium heat 5 minutes or until thoroughly heated. Stir in vinegar. Spoon ½ cup mixture over bottom half of each bun, and cover sandwiches with remaining bun halves. Yield: 6 servings (serving size: 1 sandwich).

***POINTS* value: 4**

per serving:
CALORIES 206
FAT 4.4g (saturated fat 0.5g)
PROTEIN 9.9g
CARBOHYDRATE 34.9g
FIBER 5g
CHOLESTEROL 0mg
IRON 2.7mg
SODIUM 776mg
CALCIUM 69mg

TIP: Dry mustard is made by grinding whole mustard seeds into a fine powder. It has a spicy flavor that adds a little zip to sauces, salad dressings, and main dishes.

prep: 8 minutes ∞ **cook:** 6 minutes

Soft Tacos

pictured on page 114

Our "meaty" vegetarian recipe gets its spicy seasoning from chili powder, cumin, green chiles, and fresh salsa. It contains half the fat and saturated fat of a fast-food beef soft taco.

***POINTS* value: 3**

per serving:
CALORIES 167
FAT 3.5g (saturated fat 1g)
PROTEIN 9g
CARBOHYDRATE 24g
FIBER 2.4g
CHOLESTEROL 5mg
IRON 0.8mg
SODIUM 567mg
CALCIUM 64mg

TIP: Look for fresh salsa in the produce section of your supermarket. It generally has 50% less sodium than bottled salsa, and it tastes like it's homemade.

- 2 cups frozen **meatless burger crumbles** (such as Morningstar Farms)
- 1 cup refrigerated fresh salsa
- 1/4 teaspoon chili powder
- 1/4 teaspoon ground cumin
- 1/2 cup frozen chopped onion
- 1 (4.5-ounce) can chopped green chiles, drained
- 8 (6-inch) flour tortillas
- 1/2 cup (2 ounces) reduced-fat shredded sharp Cheddar cheese or preshredded reduced-fat 4-cheese Mexican blend cheese
- 1 (14.5-ounce) can diced tomatoes, drained
- 1 1/2 cups shredded iceberg lettuce

1. Combine first 6 ingredients in a nonstick skillet, and cook over medium heat 6 to 8 minutes or until thoroughly heated, stirring occasionally.

2. Spoon mixture evenly onto tortillas; top with cheese, tomatoes, and lettuce. Yield: 8 servings (serving size: 1 taco).

prep: 2 minutes ∞ **cook:** 40 minutes

Veggie Chili

There's nothing more comforting than the aroma of spicy chili simmering on the stove. Serve with a slice of corn bread for a meal with a *POINTS* value of 6.

2 teaspoons olive oil
1 (16-ounce) package frozen bell pepper and onion stir-fry
½ cup frozen chopped onion
½ teaspoon bottled minced garlic
1 (15-ounce) can black beans, rinsed and drained
1 (15-ounce) can chili beans in mild sauce (such as Bush's Best), undrained
1 (15-ounce) can no-salt-added tomato sauce
1 (14.5-ounce) can diced tomatoes, undrained
1 (12-ounce) package frozen **meatless burger crumbles** (such as Morningstar Farms)
1 (4.5-ounce) can chopped green chiles, drained
1 tablespoon chili powder
1 teaspoon dried thyme
½ teaspoon ground cumin
½ teaspoon garlic powder
Reduced-fat sour cream (optional)

1. Heat oil in a large skillet. Add stir-fry, onion, and garlic; cook over medium-high heat 3 minutes.

2. Add black beans and next 9 ingredients, and mix well. Bring to a boil; reduce heat to medium-low. Simmer 30 minutes, stirring occasionally. Serve with sour cream, if desired. Yield: 9 servings (serving size: about 1 cup).

***POINTS* value: 3**

per serving:
CALORIES 170
FAT 3.6g (saturated fat 0.3g)
PROTEIN 11g
CARBOHYDRATE 25g
FIBER 6.8g
CHOLESTEROL 0mg
IRON 3.1mg
SODIUM 593mg
CALCIUM 50mg

TIP: Garlic powder is made by grinding dehydrated garlic flakes and is a convenient pantry item to use in sauces, rubs, and quick-and-easy dishes.

prep: 3 minutes ∞ **cook:** 16 minutes

Southwestern Chicken Pizza

pictured on page 118

You won't use a whole can of refried beans in this recipe, so refrigerate the rest to serve with baked or light tortilla chips as a snack later in the week. For a little more heat, substitute spicy refried beans.

***POINTS* value: 4**

per serving:
CALORIES 203
FAT 5.3g (saturated fat 2.2g)
PROTEIN 16.2g
CARBOHYDRATE 22.4g
FIBER 1.6g
CHOLESTEROL 22mg
IRON 1.8mg
SODIUM 521mg
CALCIUM 163mg

TIP: To shred cooked chicken, simply take two forks and pull the meat apart into bite-sized pieces. For freezing directions, see page 20.

1 (10-ounce) Italian cheese-flavored thin pizza crust (such as Boboli)
Cooking spray
1 cup refried beans
1 (4.5-ounce) can chopped green chiles, drained
1½ cups frozen shredded Versatile Baked Chicken Breast (page 20), thawed
1 cup (4 ounces) preshredded reduced-fat Mexican blend cheese
½ cup refrigerated fresh salsa
Chopped green onions
Chopped fresh cilantro

1. Preheat oven to 475°.

2. Place pizza crust on an ungreased baking sheet; lightly coat crust with cooking spray; bake at 475° for 5 minutes.

3. Meanwhile, combine beans and chiles in a microwave-safe bowl. Microwave at HIGH 1½ minutes or until thoroughly heated.

4. Spread bean mixture evenly over baked crust. Arrange chicken over beans. Sprinkle evenly with cheese.

5. Bake at 475° for 9 minutes or until cheese melts and crust is golden. Spoon salsa onto pizza. Top with green onions and cilantro. Cut into 8 slices. Yield: 8 servings (serving size: 1 slice).

prep: 6 minutes ∞ **cook:** 10 minutes

Ham and Tomato Pizza

Savory ham and juicy tomatoes seasoned with garlic and herbs are nestled atop a cheese-covered crust, making this pizza hard to resist.

- 1 (10-ounce) **Italian cheese-flavored thin pizza crust** (such as Boboli)
- Cooking spray
- 6 tablespoons part-skim ricotta cheese
- 1 (14.5-ounce) can diced tomatoes with basil, garlic, and oregano, drained
- 1 cup (4 ounces) shredded mozzarella and Asiago with roasted garlic cheese blend (such as Sargento)
- ¾ cup diced or chopped ham
- Chopped fresh basil (optional)

1. Preheat oven to 450°.

2. Place pizza crust on an ungreased baking sheet; lightly coat crust with cooking spray. Spread ricotta cheese over crust. Arrange tomatoes evenly over ricotta. Sprinkle with cheese blend; top with ham.

3. Bake at 450° for 10 minutes or until lightly browned. Sprinkle with fresh basil, if desired. Cut into 8 slices. Yield: 8 servings (serving size: 1 slice).

***POINTS* value: 4**

per serving:
CALORIES 185
FAT 5.8g (saturated fat 2.7g)
PROTEIN 11.4g
CARBOHYDRATE 21.9g
FIBER 0.9g
CHOLESTEROL 18mg
IRON 1.7mg
SODIUM 530mg
CALCIUM 190mg

TIP: Spraying the pizza crust with cooking spray before baking the crust gives it a golden color and a crisp texture.

prep: 6 minutes ⚭ **cook:** 11 minutes

Polynesian Pizza

Sweet pineapple and savory ham pair up to give this unique pizza a tasty tropical twist.

***POINTS* value: 4**

per serving:
CALORIES 186
FAT 5.4g (saturated fat 2g)
PROTEIN 10.4g
CARBOHYDRATE 23g
FIBER 1.1g
CHOLESTEROL 16mg
IRON 1.6mg
SODIUM 493mg
CALCIUM 152mg

TIP: Frozen chopped onion is a huge time-saver when you're in a hurry. Look for it alongside other vegetables in the frozen-foods section of your grocery store.

1 (10-ounce) **Italian cheese-flavored thin pizza crust** (such as Boboli)
Cooking spray
½ cup tomato-basil pasta sauce
½ cup frozen chopped onion
1 teaspoon bottled minced garlic
1 (8-ounce) can pineapple chunks in juice, drained
½ cup diced ham
1 cup (4 ounces) shredded part-skim mozzarella cheese
Crushed red pepper (optional)

1. Preheat oven to 450°.

2. Place pizza crust on an ungreased baking sheet; lightly coat crust with cooking spray. Spread pasta sauce evenly over crust; set aside.

3. Heat a large nonstick skillet over medium heat; coat pan with cooking spray. Add onion and garlic; sauté 3 minutes or until tender. Spread mixture evenly over crust. Top with pineapple chunks, diced ham, mozzarella cheese, and if desired, crushed red pepper.

4. Bake pizza at 450° for 8 to 10 minutes or until crust is crisp and cheese melts. Cut into 8 slices. Yield: 8 servings (serving size: 1 slice).

prep: 4 minutes ∞ **cook:** 10 minutes

Rustic Tomato-Olive Pizza

pictured on cover

You'll never have to wait for a pizza delivery again. You can have this pizza prepared and ready to serve in half the time it takes a pizza to be delivered to your door. Our version is healthier, too. Make it kid-friendly by omitting the olives.

2 teaspoons yellow cornmeal
1 (14-ounce) Italian cheese-flavored pizza crust (such as Boboli)
Cooking spray
1 (28-ounce) can fire-roasted diced tomatoes, drained
1 cup (4 ounces) shredded mozzarella and Asiago with roasted garlic cheese blend (such as Sargento)
1/4 cup sliced pitted kalamata olives
Chopped fresh oregano

1. Preheat oven to 450°.

2. Cover a large baking sheet with parchment paper; sprinkle with cornmeal. Place pizza crust on top of cornmeal; lightly coat crust with cooking spray. Spread with tomatoes, cheese, and olives.

3. Bake at 450° for 10 minutes or until lightly browned. Sprinkle with oregano. Cut into 8 slices. Yield: 8 servings (serving size: 1 slice).

***POINTS* value: 4**

per serving:
CALORIES 211
FAT 6.2g (saturated fat 2.4g)
PROTEIN 9.2g
CARBOHYDRATE 29.2g
FIBER 1.6g
CHOLESTEROL 8mg
IRON 1.9mg
SODIUM 637mg
CALCIUM 179mg

TIP: Use parchment paper to keep your baking sheet clean and to easily transfer the cooked pizza to a cutting board for slicing.

prep: 6 minutes ∞ **cook:** 8 minutes

Olive and Rosemary Pizza

Keep the ingredients for this pizza on hand and you'll always be prepared for last-minute dinner guests. Open a bottle of wine while the pizza cooks.

***POINTS* value: 4**

per serving:
CALORIES 201
FAT 6.6g (saturated fat 2.4g)
PROTEIN 9g
CARBOHYDRATE 26.3g
FIBER 1.5g
CHOLESTEROL 8mg
IRON 1.6mg
SODIUM 417mg
CALCIUM 169mg

TIP: When substituting dried rosemary for fresh, use an equal amount.

- 1 (14-ounce) Italian cheese-flavored pizza crust (such as Boboli)
- Cooking spray
- 1 pint grape tomatoes, halved
- 1/4 cup sliced pitted kalamata olives
- 1 cup (4 ounces) shredded part-skim mozzarella cheese
- 1/2 tablespoon chopped fresh or dried rosemary
- 1/8 teaspoon freshly ground black pepper

1. Preheat oven to 450°.

2. Place pizza crust on an ungreased baking sheet. Lightly coat crust with cooking spray. Sprinkle tomato halves and remaining ingredients evenly over crust. Bake at 450° for 8 to 10 minutes or until cheese melts and crust is lightly browned. Cut into 8 slices. Yield: 8 servings (serving size: 1 slice).

Double Duty

prep: 15 minutes ∞ **cook:** 1 hour ∞ **other:** 15 minutes

Lemon-Thyme Roasted Chicken

Roast two chickens—one for tonight's dinner and a second for a meal later in the week. We recommend Easy Chicken Pot Pie (page 59) or Couscous and Chicken Salad (page 60).

***POINTS* value: 4**

per serving:
CALORIES 201
FAT 4.8g (saturated fat 1.2g)
PROTEIN 35.6g
CARBOHYDRATE 1.9g
FIBER 0.9g
CHOLESTEROL 113mg
IRON 2.6mg
SODIUM 422mg
CALCIUM 36mg

TIP: Debone the extra chicken. Then chop or shred the meat and store in an airtight container in the refrigerator for up to two days. One 3-pound chicken will provide 3 cups of cooked chopped or shredded chicken.

2 tablespoons dried thyme
6 garlic cloves, pressed
2 teaspoons black pepper
1 teaspoon salt
2 (3-pound) roasting chickens
2 lemons, halved

1. Preheat oven to 350°.

2. Combine thyme and next 3 ingredients in a small bowl.

3. Remove and discard giblets and necks from chickens. Rinse chickens with cold water; pat dry. Trim excess fat. For each chicken, starting at neck cavity, loosen skin from breast and drumsticks by inserting fingers and gently pushing between skin and meat. Rub thyme mixture underneath loosened skin. Place lemon halves inside body cavity. Tie ends of legs together with twine. Lift wing tips up and over back; tuck under chicken.

4. Place chickens, breast sides up, on a broiler pan. Insert a meat thermometer into meaty part of a thigh, making sure not to touch bone. Bake at 350° for 1 hour or until thermometer registers 165°. Remove chickens from oven; cover with foil, and let stand 15 minutes. Discard skin and lemon. Yield: 8 servings (serving size: about 4 ounces).

prep: 5 minutes ∞ cook: 45 minutes

Easy Chicken Pot Pie

With chopped cooked chicken on standby in the refrigerator, you can have this family-favorite one-dish meal ready for the oven in about 5 minutes. We reduced the calories and fat by using a low-fat baking mix, egg substitute, and fat-free milk.

- 1 (10¾-ounce) can condensed 45% reduced sodium 98% fat-free cream of mushroom soup (such as Campbell's Healthy Request), undiluted
- 1 cup fat-free milk, divided
- ¼ teaspoon salt
- ⅛ teaspoon black pepper
- 3 cups chopped Lemon-Thyme Roasted Chicken (page 58)
- 2 cups frozen mixed vegetables
- Cooking spray
- 1 cup low-fat baking mix (such as Bisquick Heart Smart)
- 2 tablespoons egg substitute

1. Preheat oven to 375°.

2. Combine soup, ½ cup milk, salt, and pepper in a medium saucepan over medium-high heat. Bring mixture to a boil; reduce heat, and simmer, uncovered, 1 minute, stirring constantly until smooth.

3. Add chicken and mixed vegetables, stirring well to combine. Return mixture to a boil; cover, reduce heat, and simmer 5 minutes, stirring occasionally. Pour into an 11 x 7–inch baking dish coated with cooking spray.

4. Lightly spoon baking mix into a dry measuring cup; level with a knife. Combine baking mix, remaining ½ cup milk, and egg substitute in a medium bowl; stir until smooth. Spoon batter into 6 equal circular portions over chicken mixture; coat batter with cooking spray. Bake, uncovered, at 375° for 30 minutes; coat with cooking spray a second time, and bake an additional 5 minutes or until golden. Yield: 6 servings (serving size: about ¾ cup chicken mixture and 1 biscuit).

***POINTS* value: 7**

per serving:
CALORIES 339
FAT 13.2g (saturated fat 3.4g)
PROTEIN 26.6g
CARBOHYDRATE 27.1g
FIBER 3.3g
CHOLESTEROL 71mg
IRON 2.7mg
SODIUM 750mg
CALCIUM 207mg

TIP: Coating the batter with cooking spray before baking and again near the end of the baking time helps the batter develop a rich golden brown color.

prep: 12 minutes ∞ **cook:** 6 minutes ∞ **other:** 5 minutes

Couscous and Chicken Salad

pictured on page 120

Combine chicken, grapes, and fresh arugula with fluffy, tender couscous for a warm or cold one-dish meal.

***POINTS* value: 5**

per serving:
CALORIES 252
FAT 10.7g (saturated fat 2.1g)
PROTEIN 14.5g
CARBOHYDRATE 27g
FIBER 3.9g
CHOLESTEROL 34mg
IRON 1.4mg
SODIUM 431mg
CALCIUM 42mg

TIP: Most arugula from grocery stores has short, tender stems. If you buy yours in bulk or from a farmers' market, however, it might have longer, thicker stems. Trim these away by cutting them off at the base of the leaves.

- ¾ cup uncooked couscous
- 1 cup fat-free, less-sodium chicken broth
- ½ teaspoon grated fresh lemon rind
- ¼ cup fresh lemon juice
- 4 teaspoons olive oil
- 2 teaspoons honey
- ½ teaspoon salt
- ½ teaspoon freshly ground black pepper
- 1½ cups shredded Lemon-Thyme Roasted Chicken (page 58)
- 1 cup halved red grapes
- ½ cup chopped celery
- ⅓ cup chopped red onion
- 3 cups loosely packed arugula, chopped
- 2 tablespoons chopped pecans, toasted

1. Cook couscous according to package directions using chicken broth instead of water and omitting salt and fat. Fluff couscous lightly with a fork; set aside.

2. Combine lemon rind and next 5 ingredients in a small bowl; set aside.

3. Combine couscous, chicken, and next 4 ingredients in a large serving bowl. Just before serving, drizzle salad with dressing, toss to coat, and sprinkle with toasted pecans. Yield: 6 servings (serving size: 1¼ cups).

prep: 13 minutes ∞ **cook:** 16 minutes

Picadillo

The sweet and savory flavors of this Cuban dish intensify overnight, making this an ideal recipe for leftovers. Serve half of this recipe over steamed rice the first night you make it and reserve the other half to make Picadillo-Stuffed Peppers (page 62) or Picadillo Pockets (page 63) another night.

- 1 cup chopped onion
- 2 garlic cloves, minced
- ½ cup chopped green bell pepper
- 2 pounds ground round
- 2 (14.5-ounce) cans diced tomatoes with onion and green bell pepper, undrained
- 2 tablespoons tomato paste
- ¼ cup golden raisins
- ¼ cup chopped pimiento-stuffed olives
- 1 teaspoon ground cinnamon
- 1 teaspoon ground cumin
- 1 teaspoon salt
- ½ teaspoon black pepper
- ¼ cup slivered almonds, toasted

1. Sauté first 4 ingredients in a large nonstick skillet over medium-high heat until vegetables are tender and beef is browned, stirring to crumble beef. Drain well.

2. Stir in diced tomatoes and remaining ingredients. Bring to a boil; reduce heat, and simmer, uncovered, 5 minutes. Yield: 8 servings (serving size: about ⅔ cup).

***POINTS* value: 5**

per serving:
CALORIES 231
FAT 7g (saturated fat 1.7g)
PROTEIN 26.3g
CARBOHYDRATE 16.5g
FIBER 3.1g
CHOLESTEROL 60mg
IRON 2.6mg
SODIUM 873mg
CALCIUM 38mg

TIP: About 2⅔ cups of **Picadillo** and 2 cups of cooked rice will serve four and have a ***POINTS*** value of 6 per serving.

prep: 10 minutes ∞ **cook:** 30 minutes

Picadillo-Stuffed Peppers

When you sprinkle cheese over a bell pepper stuffed with Picadillo (page 61) and rice, you get an irresistible and satisfying dish. For extra heat, we added a little ground red pepper. Serve with boiled corn on the cob for a meal with a *POINTS* value of 9 per serving.

***POINTS* value: 8**

per serving:
CALORIES 388
FAT 10g (saturated fat 3.3g)
PROTEIN 31g
CARBOHYDRATE 44.9g
FIBER 6.4g
CHOLESTEROL 68mg
IRON 4.7mg
SODIUM 929mg
CALCIUM 111mg

TIP: Store unwashed, uncut fresh peppers in a plastic bag in the refrigerator. They will keep for about a week, depending on how fresh they were when purchased.

- 4 large green bell peppers
- 2⅔ cups Picadillo (page 61)
- ½ teaspoon ground red pepper
- 2 cups cooked rice
- ¼ cup (1 ounce) shredded Monterey Jack or Manchego cheese

1. Preheat oven to 425°.

2. Cut off tops of bell peppers; discard seeds and membranes. Place bell peppers, cut sides up, in an 8-inch baking dish. Microwave, uncovered, at HIGH 6 minutes or just until peppers are tender. Drain peppers, and return to dish.

3. Place Picadillo in a microwave-safe bowl; cover with heavy-duty plastic wrap, turning back an edge to vent. Microwave at HIGH 4 minutes or until hot, stirring after 2 minutes. Stir in red pepper and rice. Spoon stuffing evenly into bell peppers, and sprinkle evenly with cheese.

4. Bake at 425° for 20 minutes or until golden brown. Yield: 4 servings (serving size: 1 stuffed pepper).

prep: 10 minutes ∞ **cook:** 15 minutes

Picadillo Pockets

Spend time with your family by getting them involved in dinner preparation. Kids can use a pizza cutter to cut the dough into rectangles and then seal the pockets closed by pressing the edges with a fork. You'll feel good that these pockets have less fat and calories than traditional store-bought versions.

1 (13.8-ounce) can refrigerated pizza crust dough (such as Pillsbury)
2⅔ cups Picadillo (page 61)
Butter-flavored cooking spray

1. Preheat oven to 425°.

2. Roll out dough to a 16 x 12–inch rectangle. Cut into 8 (6 x 4–inch) rectangles.

3. Spoon about ⅓ cup Picadillo onto center of each rectangle. Fold dough over filling to form 4 x 3–inch pockets; pinch edges together with fingers. Transfer to a large ungreased baking sheet; press edges of pockets with a fork to seal. Coat pockets with cooking spray.

4. Bake at 425° for 15 minutes or until browned. Yield: 8 pockets (serving size: 1 pocket).

***POINTS* value: 5**

per serving:
CALORIES 237
FAT 5.2g (saturated fat 1.2g)
PROTEIN 16.9g
CARBOHYDRATE 31.6g
FIBER 1.5g
CHOLESTEROL 30mg
IRON 2.7mg
SODIUM 790mg
CALCIUM 19mg

TIP: These savory pockets can be frozen for up to two weeks. To freeze, assemble the pockets, and place them on a baking sheet lined with wax paper. Freeze until firm. Transfer to a large zip-top freezer bag. Bake, without thawing, at 425° for 17 minutes or until browned.

prep: 4 minutes ∞ **cook:** 18 minutes ∞ **other:** 8 hours and 10 minutes

Spicy Grilled Flank Steak with Peppers and Onions

Begin marinating this steak the evening before you plan to cook it. When you come home from work the next day, you'll have a tasty steak ready in about 20 minutes. Before serving, reserve half of the grilled steak and vegetables to make either the Grilled Flank Steak Fajita Salad (page 65) or Flank Steak Fajita Wraps (page 66).

***POINTS* value: 5**

per serving:
CALORIES 202
FAT 7.9g (saturated fat 2.4g)
PROTEIN 24.9g
CARBOHYDRATE 6.4g
FIBER 0.9g
CHOLESTEROL 39mg
IRON 1.9mg
SODIUM 353mg
CALCIUM 33mg

TIP: If you have a grill basket, use it to hold the vegetables while they grill.

- ½ cup salt-free Southwestern chipotle marinade (such as Mrs. Dash 10-Minute Marinade)
- ½ cup light Mexican beer (such as Corona Light)
- 2 tablespoons fresh lime juice
- ¾ teaspoon salt
- 2 pounds flank steak
- 1 red bell pepper, seeded and quartered
- 1 green bell pepper, seeded and quartered
- 1 large onion, cut into ½-inch-thick slices
- 1 teaspoon canola oil
- ¼ teaspoon salt
- ¼ teaspoon black pepper
- Cooking spray

1. Combine first 4 ingredients in a small bowl; reserve ¼ cup marinade for basting. Pour remaining marinade in a large zip-top plastic bag. Add steak to bag; seal bag, and marinate in refrigerator at least 8 hours, turning bag occasionally.

2. Prepare grill.

3. Combine red bell pepper and next 5 ingredients in a large bowl; toss to coat vegetables.

4. Remove steak from bag. Discard marinade. Place steak, bell peppers, and onion on grill rack coated with cooking spray. Cover and grill steak 9 minutes on each side or until desired degree of doneness, basting once with reserved ¼ cup marinade. Grill onions and bell peppers 7 minutes on each side or until done, basting once with reserved marinade.

5. Remove vegetables from grill; cut bell pepper into ¼-inch-thick slices. Set aside, and keep warm. Remove steak from grill, and let stand 10 minutes; cut diagonally across grain into thin slices. If desired, reserve half of steak and vegetables for other recipes. Yield: 8 servings (serving size: 3 ounces steak and ¼ cup grilled vegetables).

prep: 6 minutes

Grilled Flank Steak Fajita Salad

pictured on page 34

Serve this 6-minute main-dish salad with baked tortilla chips for a total *POINTS* value of 7. End the meal with Piña Colada Granita (page 181), which has a *POINTS* value of 1.

7 cups romaine lettuce
12 ounces Spicy Grilled Flank Steak and 1 cup Peppers and Onions (page 64)
1 cup refrigerated fresh salsa
1/4 cup reduced-fat sour cream
1/4 cup chopped cilantro

1. Divide lettuce among plates; top evenly with steak and vegetables.

2. Spoon salsa and sour cream evenly over salads; sprinkle with cilantro. Yield: 4 servings (serving size: 3 ounces steak, 1/4 cup vegetables, 1 3/4 cups lettuce, 1/4 cup salsa, and 1 tablespoon sour cream).

***POINTS* value: 5**

per serving:
CALORIES 262
FAT 10g (saturated fat 3.6g)
PROTEIN 26.8g
CARBOHYDRATE 12.6g
FIBER 3g
CHOLESTEROL 46mg
IRON 2.9mg
SODIUM 520mg
CALCIUM 91mg

TIP: To chop cilantro easily, place the leaves in a measuring cup, and snip with kitchen shears.

prep: 10 minutes

Flank Steak Fajita Wraps

For the ultimate quick and easy dinner, wrap Spicy Grilled Flank Steak with Peppers and Onions in blankets of warm tortillas, and top with lettuce, salsa, cheese, and sour cream.

***POINTS* value: 8**

per serving:
CALORIES 374
FAT 11.9g (saturated fat 4.7g)
PROTEIN 31.6g
CARBOHYDRATE 32.6g
FIBER 3.3g
CHOLESTEROL 52mg
IRON 2.1mg
SODIUM 741mg
CALCIUM 116mg

TIP: When a recipe calls for Cheddar cheese, use sharp or extrasharp. The sharper the Cheddar, the stronger the flavor. You can use less cheese, saving on fat grams and calories, and get the same amount of flavor.

- 1/4 cup reduced-fat sour cream
- 4 (8-inch) flour tortillas
- 12 ounces Spicy Grilled Flank Steak and 1 cup Peppers and Onions (page 64)
- 1 cup shredded romaine lettuce
- 1/4 cup (1 ounce) reduced-fat shredded sharp Cheddar cheese
- 1/4 cup refrigerated fresh salsa

1. Spread 1 tablespoon sour cream over each tortilla; top each tortilla evenly with flank steak, vegetables, lettuce, cheese, and salsa. Roll up tortillas, and cut in half. Secure each half with a wooden pick, if desired. Yield: 4 servings (serving size: 2 halves).

prep: 7 minutes ∞ **cook:** 35 minutes ∞ **other:** 10 minutes

Peach-Glazed Pork Tenderloin

Peach preserves, Dijon mustard, and low-sodium soy sauce yield a richly seasoned dish. Serve one tenderloin with Asparagus with Balsamic Butter (page 158) for a meal with a *POINTS* value of 4 per serving. Leftovers are perfect in Sweet-and-Sour Pork Lo Mein (page 68) and Barbecue Pork Baked Potatoes (page 69).

- 2 (1-pound) pork tenderloins
- ½ teaspoon salt
- ½ teaspoon freshly ground black pepper
- ½ cup peach preserves
- 1 tablespoon Dijon mustard
- 2 teaspoons low-sodium soy sauce

1. Preheat oven to 350°.

2. Place pork on a broiler pan lined with foil. Sprinkle pork with salt and pepper.

3. Combine peach preserves, mustard, and soy sauce. Brush glaze evenly over pork.

4. Bake at 350° for 35 to 45 minutes or until a meat thermometer inserted into thickest part of pork registers 155°, basting every 10 minutes. Let pork rest 10 minutes to reach 160°. Yield: 8 servings (serving size: 3 ounces).

***POINTS* value: 4**

per serving:
CALORIES 187
FAT 3.9g (saturated fat 1.3g)
PROTEIN 23.9g
CARBOHYDRATE 13.2g
FIBER 0g
CHOLESTEROL 74mg
IRON 1.4mg
SODIUM 271mg
CALCIUM 6mg

TIP: Pork tenderloin comes from the sirloin (the back part of the loin) and is the leanest and most tender cut of pork.

prep: 6 minutes ∞ **cook:** 20 minutes

Sweet-and-Sour Pork Lo Mein

Wait until everyone is ready to eat before adding the hot cooked noodles to the pork and vegetable mixture. Toss quickly, making sure the noodles are thoroughly coated with the rich brown sauce.

***POINTS* value: 5**

per serving:
CALORIES 256
FAT 4.2g (saturated fat 1g)
PROTEIN 15.1g
CARBOHYDRATE 40.1g
FIBER 2.5g
CHOLESTEROL 35mg
IRON 2.5mg
SODIUM 330mg
CALCIUM 22mg

TIP: Lo mein noodles come in various sizes and can be either flat or round. Look for them in the Asian-food section of your supermarket.

8 ounces uncooked thin lo mein noodles
1 tablespoon grated peeled fresh ginger
2 tablespoons hoisin sauce
1 tablespoon low-sodium soy sauce
1 tablespoon rice wine vinegar
2 teaspoons sesame oil
¼ cup less-sodium beef broth
1 teaspoon canola or peanut oil
Cooking spray
1 (8-ounce) package presliced mushrooms
1 cup snow peas
½ cup shredded carrot
1 (1-pound) **Peach-Glazed Pork Tenderloin** (page 67), thinly sliced
½ cup sliced green onions

1. Cook lo mein noodles according to package directions, omitting salt and fat; set aside.

2. Combine ginger and next 5 ingredients in a small bowl; set aside.

3. Heat vegetable oil in a large nonstick skillet coated with cooking spray over medium heat. Add mushrooms; sauté 4 to 5 minutes or until golden brown. Add snow peas and carrot. Sauté 3 minutes or until tender. Stir in ginger sauce and pork. Cook 1 to 2 minutes or until thoroughly heated. Toss with lo mein noodles; sprinkle each serving with green onions. Serve immediately. Yield: 7 servings (serving size: 1 cup).

prep: 5 minutes ∞ **cook:** 48 minutes

Barbecue Pork Baked Potatoes

With minimal prep time, these cheesy barbecue pork–stuffed spuds can be oven-ready in minutes and will definitely please everyone in the family.

6 (6-ounce) baking potatoes
1 (1-pound) Peach-Glazed Pork Tenderloin (page 67), chopped
⅓ cup smoky-flavored barbecue sauce
6 tablespoons reduced-fat shredded sharp Cheddar cheese
½ cup fat-free sour cream
¼ cup sliced green onions

1. Preheat oven to 450°.

2. Bake potatoes at 450° for 45 minutes or until done; cool slightly.

3. Combine chopped pork and barbecue sauce in a large saucepan over medium heat. Cook 3 minutes or until warm.

4. Cut a slit in each potato. Top evenly with pork, cheese, sour cream, and green onions. Serve immediately. Yield: 6 servings (serving size: 1 potato, ⅓ cup (about 3 ounces) pork, 1 tablespoon cheese, and about 1 tablespoon sour cream).

***POINTS* value: 6**

per serving:
CALORIES 304
FAT 4.1g (saturated fat 1.9g)
PROTEIN 18.8g
CARBOHYDRATE 48.2g
FIBER 3.6g
CHOLESTEROL 47mg
IRON 2.8mg
SODIUM 355mg
CALCIUM 92mg

TIP: Reduce the cook time by microwaving the potatoes. Pierce the potatoes with a fork; arrange in a circle on paper towels in the microwave oven. Microwave at HIGH 16 minutes or until done, rearranging after 8 minutes. Let the potatoes stand 5 minutes.

prep: 10 minutes ∞ **cook:** 12 minutes

Grilled Vegetables

The subtle sweetness of veggies is enhanced when they're grilled, which makes this simple recipe a delicious side to serve with Grilled Swordfish Steaks with Sun-Dried Tomato Butter (page 95). Use the leftover vegetables to make Tortelloni with Grilled Vegetables (page 71) or Grilled-Vegetable Hoagies with Basil Mayonnaise (page 72).

***POINTS* value: 1**

per serving:
CALORIES 46
FAT 1.5g (saturated fat 0.2g)
PROTEIN 1.9g
CARBOHYDRATE 7.9g
FIBER 2.3g
CHOLESTEROL 0mg
IRON 0.5mg
SODIUM 108mg
CALCIUM 25mg

TIP: To use your leftovers in either of the following two recipes, you'll need to reserve 4 cups of the veggies to make the tortelloni dish or 3 cups to make the sandwiches.

1 red bell pepper
1 large eggplant, cut lengthwise into 1/4-inch-thick slices
2 medium zucchini, cut lengthwise into 1/4-inch-thick slices
3 yellow squash, cut lengthwise into 1/4-inch-thick slices
1 medium sweet onion, cut into 1/2-inch-thick slices
Cooking spray
1 tablespoon olive oil
1/2 teaspoon salt
1/2 teaspoon black pepper
1 teaspoon dried Italian seasoning

1. Prepare grill.

2. Cut bell pepper in half lengthwise; discard seeds and membranes. Place bell pepper halves, skin sides up, on a flat surface; flatten with hand. Coat all vegetables on both sides with cooking spray.

3. Grill vegetables 12 to 15 minutes or just until tender, turning after 8 minutes. Coarsely chop vegetables into 1-inch pieces. Combine olive oil and next 3 ingredients in a large bowl, stirring well. Add vegetables, and toss to coat. Yield: 6 cups (serving size: 1/2 cup).

prep: 4 minutes ∞ **cook:** 13 minutes

Tortelloni with Grilled Vegetables

pictured on page 43

This quick pasta dish gets its depth of flavor from fresh basil and freshly grated Parmesan cheese.

- 2 (14.5-ounce) jars petite diced tomatoes (such as Del Monte Garden Select), undrained
- 1/4 teaspoon freshly ground black pepper
- 1 (9-ounce) package fresh portobello mushroom and cheese tortelloni (such as Buitoni)
- 4 cups **Grilled Vegetables** (page 70)
- 1/3 cup chopped fresh basil
- 6 tablespoons freshly grated Parmesan cheese

1. Combine tomatoes and black pepper in a 4-quart saucepan; bring to a boil over medium-high heat. Gently stir in tortelloni. Cover, reduce heat, and simmer 6 minutes.

2. Gently stir in Grilled Vegetables and basil. Cook 2 minutes or just until vegetables are thoroughly heated. Sprinkle each serving with cheese, and serve immediately. Yield: 6 servings (serving size: 1 1/3 cups pasta mixture and 1 tablespoon cheese).

***POINTS* value: 4**

per serving:
CALORIES 235
FAT 6.5g (saturated fat 2.3g)
PROTEIN 10g
CARBOHYDRATE 37.5g
FIBER 5.5g
CHOLESTEROL 16mg
IRON 1.9mg
SODIUM 877mg
CALCIUM 150mg

TIP: For a variation, substitute refrigerated fresh cheese ravioli.

prep: 6 minutes ∞ **cook:** 12 minutes

Grilled-Vegetable Hoagies with Basil Mayonnaise

Creamy basil mayonnaise is slathered on whole wheat hoagie rolls and combined with melted cheese to transform these grilled vegetables into a hearty vegetarian sandwich that's great for a quick lunch or dinner. Serve with 1 cup of fresh orange sections for a meal with a *POINTS* value of 9 per serving.

***POINTS* value: 8**

per serving:
CALORIES 363
FAT 13.4g (saturated fat 5.6g)
PROTEIN 17.9g
CARBOHYDRATE 47.1g
FIBER 5.5g
CHOLESTEROL 11mg
IRON 1.9mg
SODIUM 739mg
CALCIUM 349mg

TIP: To chop basil, stack the leaves, roll them cigar-style, and cut the roll into thin slices.

- 3 cups Grilled Vegetables (page 70)
- 1/4 cup light mayonnaise
- 2 tablespoons chopped fresh basil
- 1/2 teaspoon lemon juice
- 1/8 teaspoon salt
- 1/8 teaspoon black pepper
- 4 (6-inch) whole wheat hoagie rolls, halved lengthwise
- 4 (.85-ounce) slices reduced-fat Swiss-style cheese (such as Jarlsburg Lite)

1. Preheat oven to 300°.

2. Place Grilled Vegetables in a microwave-safe bowl. Microwave, uncovered, at HIGH for 1½ to 2 minutes or until thoroughly heated.

3. Stir together mayonnaise and next 4 ingredients in a small bowl; spread on cut sides of rolls.

4. Spoon about 3/4 cup Grilled Vegetables on bottom halves of each roll; top each with a slice of cheese. Cover with top halves of rolls. Place rolls on a baking sheet.

5. Bake at 300° for 10 minutes or until cheese melts. Yield: 4 servings (serving size: 1 sandwich).

Slow Cooker

prep: 18 minutes ∞ **cook:** 6 hours ∞ **other:** 10 minutes

Chinese Chicken with Garlic-Sauced Noodles

Why call for take-out Chinese food when you can create a healthier meal at home? Here, chicken thighs simmer in a dark syrupy mixture that's reminiscent of a sweet barbecue sauce. Then the chicken is tossed with hot cooked noodles flavored with rice wine vinegar and dark sesame oil.

***POINTS* value: 8**

per serving:
CALORIES 389
FAT 14.6g (saturated fat 3.4g)
PROTEIN 30.1g
CARBOHYDRATE 33.2g
FIBER 2.6g
CHOLESTEROL 85mg
IRON 2.7mg
SODIUM 598mg
CALCIUM 37mg

TIP: Put the water for the pasta on to boil just before you remove the chicken from the cooker to let it stand for 10 minutes. For 8 ounces of dried pasta, you'll need a 4-quart pot. Cover the pot, and bring the water to a full rolling boil over high heat before adding the pasta.

2 pounds boneless, skinless chicken thighs
Cooking spray
1 tablespoon hoisin sauce
1 tablespoon low-sodium soy sauce
1 teaspoon sugar
2 teaspoons bottled minced garlic
1 teaspoon bottled minced ginger
1/4 cup low-sodium soy sauce
1/4 cup rice wine vinegar
1 teaspoon dark sesame oil
4 cups cooked vermicelli (about 8 ounces uncooked)
1 cup matchstick-cut carrots
3/4 cup diagonally sliced green onions (about 3)
1/2 cup chopped fresh cilantro, divided
1/3 cup chopped unsalted, dry-roasted peanuts

1. Place chicken thighs in a 4-quart electric slow cooker coated with cooking spray. Combine hoisin sauce and next 4 ingredients; stir well, and drizzle over chicken thighs. Cover and cook on HIGH 1 hour. Reduce heat to LOW, and cook 5 hours.

2. Remove chicken from cooker, and place in a large bowl; let stand 10 minutes. Reserve cooking liquid.

3. Shred chicken with 2 forks. Combine chicken and 1/4 cup reserved cooking liquid; toss to coat, and set aside. In a large bowl, combine remaining cooking liquid, 1/4 cup soy sauce, vinegar, and sesame oil. Add pasta, carrots, green onions, and 1/4 cup cilantro; toss to coat. Add chicken, and toss well.

4. Sprinkle with peanuts and remaining 1/4 cup chopped cilantro. Yield: 7 servings (serving size: about 1 cup).

prep: 15 minutes ∞ **cook:** 6 hours

Stewed Chicken Thighs with Sweet Potatoes

This aromatic one-dish meal will bring your family running to the table as soon as you take the lid off the slow cooker. For heartier fare, serve over ½ cup of hot cooked couscous for a total *POINTS* value of 10 per serving.

- 2 medium sweet potatoes, peeled and cubed (about 1 pound unpeeled)
- ¾ cup chopped onion
- ¼ cup dried apricots, chopped
- ¼ cup raisins
- 1½ tablespoons brown sugar
- 1 teaspoon bottled minced garlic
- ¾ cup fat-free, less-sodium chicken broth
- 1½ pounds skinless, boneless chicken thighs
- 1¼ teaspoons curry powder
- ½ teaspoon salt
- ¼ teaspoon ground cumin
- ¼ teaspoon ground cinnamon
- ¼ teaspoon black pepper

1. Combine first 6 ingredients in a 4- to 5-quart electric slow cooker; pour broth over vegetables. Arrange chicken thighs over vegetables; sprinkle with remaining ingredients.

2. Cover and cook on HIGH 1 hour. Reduce heat to LOW; cook 5 hours. To serve, spoon vegetable mixture and juices over chicken thighs. Yield: 4 servings (serving size: 2 chicken thighs and ¾ cup vegetable mixture).

***POINTS* value: 8**

per serving:
CALORIES 400
FAT 13.2g (saturated fat 3.6g)
PROTEIN 33.4g
CARBOHYDRATE 36.1g
FIBER 4.3g
CHOLESTEROL 112mg
IRON 3.1mg
SODIUM 532mg
CALCIUM 64mg

TIP: Dried apricots can be frustrating to chop because they are sticky and tend to clump together. Spray your knife or kitchen shears with cooking spray before chopping.

prep: 7 minutes ∞ **cook:** 6 hours and 7 minutes

Turkey and Black Bean Chili

Regular ground turkey is a combination of white and dark meat and is higher in fat than ground turkey breast. We prefer the added flavor that the mix of dark and white meat gives to this hearty chili. If you want a leaner chili, use ground turkey breast for a *POINTS* value of 3 per serving.

***POINTS* value: 4**

per serving:
CALORIES 220
FAT 7g (saturated fat 2.8g)
PROTEIN 20.6g
CARBOHYDRATE 23.1g
FIBER 6.7g
CHOLESTEROL 52mg
IRON 2.3mg
SODIUM 635mg
CALCIUM 99mg

TIP: Always fill a slow cooker at least half full and no more than two-thirds full. The food level you start with is important in order for food to cook properly; it's okay if food cooks down. If you can't find a mixture of prechopped onion and bell pepper in your produce section, use 1 cup chopped of each.

Cooking spray
1¼ pounds ground turkey
2 cups prechopped onion and bell pepper mix
1 (15-ounce) can seasoned diced tomato sauce for chili (such as Hunt's)
1 (14.5-ounce) can no-salt-added diced tomatoes, undrained
2 (15-ounce) cans 50%-less-sodium black beans (such as S&W), rinsed and drained
1 tablespoon chili powder
⅛ teaspoon ground red pepper
½ cup reduced-fat sour cream

1. Heat a large nonstick skillet over medium-high heat; coat pan with cooking spray. Add turkey and onion and bell pepper mix; cook until turkey is browned, stirring to crumble. Drain.

2. Combine turkey mixture, tomato sauce, and next 4 ingredients in a 4-quart electric slow cooker. Cover and cook on LOW 6 hours. Ladle chili into bowls; top with sour cream. Yield: 8 servings (serving size: 1 cup chili and 1 tablespoon sour cream).

prep: 4 minutes ∞ **cook:** 6 hours ∞ **other:** 20 minutes

Jerk Turkey Soup ☑

This soup holds well in the slow cooker, so plan to serve it on a night when everyone in your family is on a different schedule. After the soup has finished cooking, turn the slow cooker to the lowest setting, and place bowls next to the cooker so that everyone can serve themselves.

1 pound boneless, skinless turkey breasts, cut into 1-inch pieces
2 teaspoons salt-free Jamaican jerk seasoning
1 medium onion, chopped
1 garlic clove, minced
1 (14.5-ounce) can diced tomatoes with zesty mild green chiles, undrained
1 (15-ounce) can black beans, rinsed and drained
2 cups fat-free, less-sodium chicken broth
1/4 teaspoon salt
2 tablespoons minced fresh cilantro
1 tablespoon fresh lime juice
Fat-free sour cream (optional)

1. Place turkey in a medium bowl; sprinkle with jerk seasoning, and toss to coat. Let stand 15 minutes.

2. Place onion in a 4- to 5-quart electric slow cooker; add turkey and spices left in bowl. Stir in garlic and next 4 ingredients. Cover and cook on HIGH 1 hour; reduce heat to LOW and cook 5 to 6 hours or until turkey is tender and done.

3. Stir in cilantro and lime juice; let stand 5 minutes. Ladle soup into bowls; top with sour cream, if desired. Yield: 6 servings (serving size: about 1 1/4 cups).

***POINTS* value: 2**

per serving:
CALORIES 141
FAT 0.5g (saturated fat 0.2g)
PROTEIN 22.3g
CARBOHYDRATE 12.4g
FIBER 3.1g
CHOLESTEROL 47mg
IRON 2mg
SODIUM 657mg
CALCIUM 39mg

TIP: Keep perishable ingredients refrigerated until you're ready to use them. Because slow cookers don't heat food as quickly as conventional appliances, it's especially important not to allow perishable food to sit out at room temperature, which allows bacteria to grow. Be sure to thaw meats completely before cooking.

prep: 12 minutes ∞ **cook:** 8 hours and 8 minutes

Beef and Vegetable Spaghetti

Convenient ingredients are quickly stirred together and slowly cooked with fresh vegetables to create this satisfying, zesty Italian meal that's perfect to serve on a busy weeknight.

***POINTS* value: 7**

per serving:
CALORIES 346
FAT 5.3g (saturated fat 2g)
PROTEIN 25.6g
CARBOHYDRATE 51.3g
FIBER 6.9g
CHOLESTEROL 38mg
IRON 5.4mg
SODIUM 563mg
CALCIUM 160mg

TIP: Browning meat before adding it to a slow cooker allows it to take on a more appealing color, and you can drain off any grease that accumulates in the pan. Also, browning quickly increases the temperature of the meat to a degree that's safe enough to prevent the growth of harmful bacteria so the dish can cook the entire time on LOW.

1½ pounds ground sirloin
1 (8-ounce) package presliced mushrooms
2 medium carrots, quartered
1 large onion, cut into 8 wedges
4 garlic cloves
2 (14.5-ounce) cans diced tomatoes with basil, garlic, and oregano, undrained
2 (6-ounce) cans no-salt-added tomato paste
4 (8-ounce) cans no-salt-added tomato sauce
1 tablespoon light brown sugar
2 teaspoons dried basil
1 teaspoon dried oregano
¼ teaspoon ground red pepper
1 (1-pound) package multigrain spaghetti (such as Barilla Plus)
⅔ cup grated Parmesan cheese

1. Place beef in a large nonstick skillet. Place mushrooms in a food processor, and process until finely minced; add to beef. Process carrot, onion, and garlic until chopped; add to beef mixture. Cook over medium-high heat 8 minutes or until beef is browned and liquid evaporates, stirring to crumble beef.

2. Place tomatoes and next 6 ingredients in a 5-quart electric slow cooker. Add beef mixture, and stir well. Cover and cook on LOW 8 hours.

3. Cook pasta according to package directions, omitting salt and fat. Drain. Serve sauce over pasta; sprinkle with Parmesan cheese. Yield: 11 servings (serving size: about 1 cup pasta, 1 cup sauce, and about 1 tablespoon cheese).

prep: 12 minutes ∞ **cook:** 9 hours

Provençal Pot Roast

With less than 15 minutes of prep time in the morning, this succulent roast is your time-saving solution when you want a comforting dinner that is simple to prepare. To reduce the prep time, look for prechopped onions and carrots in the produce section of your supermarket.

- ¾ cup chopped onion
- 2 large carrots, sliced
- 2 garlic cloves, minced
- 1 (2½-pound) sirloin tip roast, cut in half
- 1 teaspoon dried Italian seasoning
- ½ teaspoon salt
- ¼ teaspoon black pepper
- 1 (14.5-ounce) can diced tomatoes with basil, garlic, and oregano, undrained
- 1 (15.5-ounce) can cannellini beans, rinsed and drained
- 1 (8-ounce) package presliced mushrooms
- ¾ cup fat-free, less-sodium beef broth

1. Place first 3 ingredients in a 5- to 6-quart electric slow cooker. Place roast over vegetables. Sprinkle seasoning, salt, and pepper over roast. Pour tomatoes and beans over roast. Sprinkle mushrooms evenly over beans. Pour broth over all ingredients.

2. Cover and cook on HIGH 1 hour. Reduce heat to LOW, and cook 8 hours. Yield: 10 servings (serving size: about 2 ounces beef and ½ cup vegetables).

***POINTS* value: 7**

per serving:
CALORIES 291
FAT 16.6g (saturated fat 6.5g)
PROTEIN 24.4g
CARBOHYDRATE 9.9g
FIBER 2.1g
CHOLESTEROL 75mg
IRON 3.2mg
SODIUM 429mg
CALCIUM 41mg

TIP: Use an instant-read thermometer to check the internal temperature of large pieces of meat. Here are the safe temperatures to reach:
- Beef: 145° to 170°
- Lamb: 145° to 170°
- Pork: 160° to 170°
- Poultry: at least 165°

prep: 9 minutes ∞ **cook:** 8 hours and 30 minutes

Irish Beef Stew

Browning the lean beef tips before adding them to the slow cooker adds rich flavor to the stew. Cooking on LOW for a long time yields tender and juicy chunks of meat.

***POINTS* value: 7**

per serving:
CALORIES 348
FAT 9g (saturated fat 3.2g)
PROTEIN 38g
CARBOHYDRATE 26.1g
FIBER 4.5g
CHOLESTEROL 98mg
IRON 3.9mg
SODIUM 689mg
CALCIUM 44mg

TIP: Vegetables such as carrots, onions, and potatoes cook more slowly in a slow cooker than meats, so layer your veggies in the cooker before adding the meat. This will allow them to cook faster.

Cooking spray
1½ pounds beef tips, cut into 1-inch pieces
1 medium onion, chopped
5 carrots, peeled and sliced into ½-inch-thick pieces (about 2 cups)
1 (1-pound, 4-ounce) bag refrigerated red potato wedges (such as Simply Potatoes)
3 garlic cloves, minced
2 (10½-ounce) cans beef consommé
1½ cups plus 2 tablespoons water, divided
2 tablespoons tomato paste
1 teaspoon dried thyme
1 bay leaf
½ teaspoon black pepper
2 tablespoons cornstarch

1. Heat a large nonstick skillet over medium-high heat; coat pan with cooking spray. Add beef, and cook 10 to 15 minutes or until thoroughly browned on all sides.

2. While beef cooks, place onion and next 3 ingredients in a 4-quart electric slow cooker.

3. Place beef on top of vegetable mixture in cooker. Add beef consommé, 1½ cups water, tomato paste, and next 3 ingredients. Cover and cook on LOW 8 hours or until beef is tender. Discard bay leaf.

4. Combine remaining 2 tablespoons water and cornstarch in a small bowl, stirring with a whisk until smooth; stir into beef mixture in cooker. Cover quickly and increase heat to HIGH; cook 20 minutes or until gravy is thick. Yield: 6 servings (serving size: about 1½ cups).

prep: 12 minutes ◎◎ **cook:** 9 hours and 32 minutes

Balsamic and Fig–Glazed Pork Roast

A combination of balsamic vinegar and fig preserves enhances the subtle sweetness of the pork. To round out your meal, serve with ½ cup store-bought refrigerated mashed sweet potatoes and steamed green beans for a meal with a *POINTS* value of 7 per serving.

1 (3-pound) boneless pork loin roast, trimmed
¾ teaspoon salt
¼ teaspoon black pepper
Cooking spray
1 cup chopped red onion
½ cup fat-free, less-sodium chicken broth
2 large garlic cloves, minced
1½ teaspoons Italian seasoning
¼ cup balsamic vinegar
¾ cup fig preserves
2 tablespoons cornstarch
2 tablespoons water

1. Cut pork in half crosswise. Sprinkle with salt and pepper, and coat with cooking spray.

2. Heat a large nonstick skillet over medium-high heat. Add pork, and cook 12 minutes or until browned on all sides.

3. While pork cooks, place onion in a 3½-quart electric slow cooker coated with cooking spray. Combine chicken broth and next 3 ingredients in a small bowl, stirring well.

4. Remove pork from pan, and place on top of onion in cooker. Pour broth mixture into pan, stirring to loosen browned bits. Stir in preserves. Pour preserve mixture over pork. Cover and cook on LOW 9 hours. Remove pork to a serving platter. Cover and keep warm.

5. Combine cornstarch and water in a small bowl, stirring with a whisk until smooth; stir into cooking liquid in cooker. Cover quickly and increase heat to HIGH; cook 20 minutes or until gravy is thick. Yield: 12 servings (serving size: 3 ounces pork and about ⅓ cup gravy).

***POINTS* value: 5**

per serving:
CALORIES 223
FAT 6g (saturated fat 2g)
PROTEIN 25.3g
CARBOHYDRATE 14.8g
FIBER 0.2g
CHOLESTEROL 71mg
IRON 1mg
SODIUM 274mg
CALCIUM 28mg

TIP: A slurry of cornstarch and water will thicken the juices that remain in the cooker after the meat is removed, creating a flavorful gravy.

prep: 30 minutes ∞ **cook:** 5 hours and 28 minutes

Rosemary-Orange Pork Roast with Acorn Squash and Sweet Potatoes

pictured on page 117

You'll be inspired to invite friends for dinner on a weeknight with this fork-tender pork roast. Toss together a quick salad, and dinner is ready. If you have a few extra minutes, prepare Raisin Brownie Bars (page 188) for dessert.

***POINTS* value: 8**

per serving:
CALORIES 354
FAT 12.9g (saturated fat 4.5g)
PROTEIN 24.1g
CARBOHYDRATE 34.2g
FIBER 1.5g
CHOLESTEROL 68mg
IRON 1.6mg
SODIUM 293mg
CALCIUM 55mg

TIP: Like other winter squash, acorn squash has a thick rind that can be difficult to cut. Pierce the squash with a fork several times, and then microwave it at HIGH for a minute or two. Let it stand a few minutes before you cut it. Use a vegetable peeler to remove the rind.

1 small acorn squash, peeled, seeded, and cut into 2-inch pieces
2 medium sweet potatoes, peeled and cut into 2-inch pieces
1 cup chopped onion
1½ teaspoons black pepper
1 teaspoon salt
1 (3-pound) boneless pork loin roast, trimmed
1 tablespoon olive oil
1½ cups low-sugar orange marmalade (such as Smucker's)
¾ cup fat-free, less-sodium chicken broth
¼ cup orange juice
2 tablespoons chopped fresh rosemary
2 tablespoons cornstarch
2 tablespoons water
Rosemary sprigs (optional)

1. Place squash, potatoes, and onion in a 5-quart electric slow cooker.

2. Combine pepper and salt; rub mixture over pork. Heat oil in a large skillet over medium-high heat; add pork, browning on all sides. Place pork in cooker on top of vegetables.

3. Combine marmalade and next 3 ingredients in a medium bowl; pour mixture over pork and vegetables.

4. Cover and cook on LOW 5 hours.

5. Remove pork to a serving platter; cover and keep warm. Combine cornstarch and water in a small bowl, stirring with a whisk until smooth; stir into vegetables in cooker. Increase heat to HIGH; cook 20 minutes or until sauce is thick. Spoon sauce over pork. Garnish with rosemary sprigs, if desired. Yield: 12 servings (serving size: 3 ounces pork and ½ cup vegetable mixture).

Easy Entrées

prep: 15 minutes ∞ **cook:** 20 minutes

Grilled Chicken with Fresh Orange Salsa

pictured on page 33

This cool, zesty salsa captures the fresh flavors of the tropics. We've paired the salsa with grilled chicken breast, but it's delicious served with grilled fish, shrimp, pork chops, or pork tenderloin. Serve with steamed green beans and ½ cup rice with chopped green onions for a meal with a *POINTS* value of 7 per serving.

***POINTS* value: 5**

per serving:
CALORIES 268
FAT 5.8g (saturated fat 0.7g)
PROTEIN 40.1g
CARBOHYDRATE 13.8g
FIBER 1.9g
CHOLESTEROL 99mg
IRON 1.4mg
SODIUM 184mg
CALCIUM 52mg

TIP: Look for salt-free marinades near the condiments and salad dressings at your supermarket.

- ½ cup salt-free zesty garlic-herb marinade (such as Mrs. Dash)
- 4 (6-ounce) skinless, boneless chicken breast halves
- 2 oranges
- ¼ cup finely chopped onion
- 2 tablespoons chopped fresh mint
- 1 tablespoon chopped jalapeño pepper
- 1 tablespoon chopped fresh cilantro
- 1 garlic clove, minced
- ½ teaspoon olive oil
- ¼ teaspoon ground cumin
- ⅛ teaspoon salt
- ⅛ teaspoon freshly ground black pepper
- Cooking spray

1. Prepare grill.

2. Pour marinade over chicken, and let stand 10 minutes.

3. While chicken marinates, grate ¼ teaspoon rind from 1 orange; place in a small bowl. Peel and section oranges over bowl; squeeze membranes to extract juice. Discard membranes. Add onion and next 8 ingredients to orange sections and juice in bowl; toss gently.

4. Place chicken on grill rack coated with cooking spray. Grill 10 minutes on each side or until done. Serve chicken with salsa. Yield: 4 servings (serving size: 1 chicken breast half and ¼ cup salsa).

prep: 15 minutes ∞ **cook:** 9 minutes

Seared Chicken Breast with Pan Gravy

pictured on page 37

This is a lightened version of a classic family-friendly recipe. Rather than deep-fat frying, we lightly floured the chicken and then browned it in a minimal amount of olive oil to seal in the natural juices. Serve with ½ cup mashed potatoes and steamed carrots for a meal with a POINTS value of 8 per serving.

- 4 (6-ounce) skinless, boneless chicken breast halves
- 1 tablespoon chopped fresh thyme
- ½ teaspoon salt
- ¾ teaspoon coarsely ground black pepper, divided
- ¼ cup plus 1 tablespoon all-purpose flour, divided
- 1 tablespoon olive oil
- ¼ cup minced shallots (1 medium)
- 1 cup fat-free, less-sodium chicken broth
- 1 tablespoon fresh lemon juice

1. Place each chicken breast half between 2 sheets of heavy-duty plastic wrap; pound to a ¼-inch thickness using a meat mallet or small heavy skillet.

2. Sprinkle chicken with thyme, salt, and ½ teaspoon pepper. Place ¼ cup flour in a shallow dish. Dredge chicken in flour.

3. Heat oil in a large skillet over medium-high heat. Add chicken, and cook 2 to 3 minutes on each side or until done. Remove chicken from pan; keep warm. Add shallots; cook 1 minute.

4. Stir in chicken broth and remaining 1 tablespoon flour, scraping pan to loosen browned bits. Simmer 3 to 4 minutes or until gravy is reduced and slightly thick, stirring constantly. Add lemon juice and remaining ¼ teaspoon pepper. Spoon gravy over chicken. Yield: 4 servings (serving size: 1 chicken breast half and 3 tablespoons gravy).

***POINTS* value: 6**

per serving:
CALORIES 266
FAT 5.7g (saturated fat 1.1g)
PROTEIN 41.4g
CARBOHYDRATE 10.1g
FIBER 0.5g
CHOLESTEROL 99mg
IRON 1.9mg
SODIUM 545mg
CALCIUM 28mg

TIP: Pounding the chicken breast halves reduces the cooking time and makes the chicken tender and juicy.

prep: 6 minutes ∞ cook: 25 minutes

Mexican Stuffed Chicken Breasts

In this recipe, we've simplified the traditional method for stuffing chicken breasts. Not only is it easier to accomplish, but you get more stuffing with each bite of tender breast.

***POINTS* value: 5**

per serving:
CALORIES 259
FAT 3.3g (saturated fat 1.3g)
PROTEIN 44.9g
CARBOHYDRATE 10.5g
FIBER 3g
CHOLESTEROL 101mg
IRON 2.4mg
SODIUM 600mg
CALCIUM 102mg

TIP: Place chicken on a cutting board. Using a sharp knife, cut a 3-inch lengthwise slit in the thickest portion of each breast (do not cut all the way through breast). Spoon one-fourth of bean mixture into each pocket.

4 (6-ounce) skinless, boneless chicken breast halves
⅔ cup canned fat-free refried beans
¼ cup chopped fresh cilantro
1 tablespoon canned chopped green chiles
1 garlic clove, minced
¼ teaspoon ground cumin
⅛ teaspoon salt
⅛ teaspoon freshly ground black pepper
Cooking spray
½ cup bottled salsa
¼ cup preshredded reduced-fat 4-cheese Mexican blend cheese

1. Preheat oven to 400°.

2. Cut a 3-inch lengthwise slit in the thickest portion of each chicken breast half to form a pocket (do not cut all the way through the breast). Set aside.

3. Stir together beans and next 4 ingredients in a small bowl. Spoon one-fourth of bean mixture into each pocket. Sprinkle chicken evenly with salt and pepper. Place stuffed chicken breast halves on a baking sheet coated with cooking spray. Bake at 400° for 20 to 22 minutes or until chicken is done.

4. Spoon 2 tablespoons salsa evenly over each chicken breast half, and top each with 1 tablespoon cheese. Bake an additional 5 minutes or until cheese melts. Serve immediately. Yield: 4 servings (serving size: 1 chicken breast half).

prep: 10 minutes ∞ **cook:** 1 minute

Barbecue Chicken Wraps

These saucy barbecue sandwiches will satisfy the heartiest of appetites. This recipe features shredded chicken and creamy broccoli coleslaw wrapped in a whole wheat tortilla. Serve with 1 cup of cubed watermelon for a meal with a *POINTS* value of 7.

- 2 cups packaged broccoli slaw
- 3 tablespoons light coleslaw dressing (such as Marzetti)
- 1/4 teaspoon freshly ground black pepper
- 2 cups shredded cooked chicken breast
- 1/4 cup barbecue sauce (such as KC Masterpiece)
- 4 (8-inch) reduced-fat whole wheat tortillas (such as Mission 96% Fat Free Heart Healthy)

1. Combine first 3 ingredients in a medium bowl. Cover and chill until ready to assemble wraps.

2. Combine chicken and barbecue sauce in a microwave-safe bowl. Microwave at HIGH 1 minute or until thoroughly heated, stirring after 30 seconds.

3. Divide chicken mixture among tortillas; top with slaw. Roll up tortillas; place seam sides down, and cut in half crosswise, securing with wooden picks, if necessary. Serve immediately. Yield: 4 servings (serving size: 2 tortilla halves).

***POINTS* value: 6**

per serving:
CALORIES 325
FAT 6.6g (saturated fat 1.1g)
PROTEIN 26.6g
CARBOHYDRATE 39.1g
FIBER 4g
CHOLESTEROL 69mg
IRON 2.8mg
SODIUM 656mg
CALCIUM 118mg

TIP: Wrap each sandwich in parchment or wax paper to hold it together for easier slicing and eating. Parchment paper is now available in sheets and rolls in most supermarkets.

prep: 12 minutes ∞ cook: 20 minutes ∞ other: 10 minutes

Cornmeal-Crusted Chicken Fingers

pictured on page 121

It's hard to tell a difference between these faux-fried fingers and those that are deep-fried. Serve them with your family's favorite dipping sauce, such as honey mustard, marinara sauce, or low-fat ranch dressing.

***POINTS* value: 5**

per serving:
CALORIES 217
FAT 6.2g (saturated fat 1.6g)
PROTEIN 29.5g
CARBOHYDRATE 9.8g
FIBER 0.7g
CHOLESTEROL 68mg
IRON 1.7mg
SODIUM 601mg
CALCIUM 99mg

TIP: Be sure to let the chicken tenders stand for 10 minutes before you bake them. This will give you the opportunity to preheat the jelly-roll pan; a hot pan produces the crispiest crust on oven-fried chicken.

6 tablespoons yellow cornmeal
3 tablespoons preshredded Parmesan cheese
½ teaspoon salt, divided
½ teaspoon freshly ground black pepper
1 large egg white
1½ pounds chicken breast tenders
Cooking spray

1. Preheat oven to 450°.

2. Combine cornmeal, cheese, ¼ teaspoon salt, and pepper in a shallow dish. Place egg white in another shallow dish.

3. Sprinkle chicken with remaining ¼ teaspoon salt; dip chicken tenders in egg white, and then dredge in cornmeal mixture, pressing firmly to coat. Shake off excess. Place chicken on a wire rack, and let stand 10 minutes. While chicken stands, place a jelly-roll pan in oven to heat.

4. Coat chicken well with cooking spray. Remove hot pan from oven; coat with cooking spray. Place chicken on pan in a single layer. Bake at 450° for 20 to 25 minutes or until chicken is done. Yield: 4 servings (serving size: about 3 chicken tenders).

prep: 11 minutes ∞ **cook:** 6 minutes ∞ **other:** 30 minutes

Mediterranean Chicken Skewers

A cool and creamy dipping sauce made with yogurt, cucumber, and mint is a refreshing complement to grilled chicken. Serve this entrée with sliced tomatoes and small pita rounds cut into triangles.

12 (12-inch) wooden skewers
¾ cup plain low-fat yogurt
½ cup diced peeled cucumber
2 tablespoons finely chopped fresh mint
1 tablespoon olive oil, divided
½ teaspoon garlic salt, divided
1½ pounds chicken breast tenders
¼ teaspoon freshly ground black pepper

1. Soak skewers in water 30 minutes.

2. Prepare grill.

3. Combine yogurt, cucumber, mint, 2 teaspoons oil, and ¼ teaspoon garlic salt in a small bowl. Cover and chill in refrigerator at least 30 minutes to allow flavors to blend.

4. Thread chicken onto skewers. Brush with remaining 1 teaspoon olive oil, and sprinkle with remaining ¼ teaspoon garlic salt and pepper. Grill 3 to 4 minutes on each side or until done. Serve chicken with yogurt sauce. Yield: 4 servings (serving size: 3 skewers and about ¼ cup sauce).

***POINTS* value: 5**

per serving:
CALORIES 251
FAT 6.4g (saturated fat 1.5g)
PROTEIN 41.9g
CARBOHYDRATE 4.1g
FIBER 0.4g
CHOLESTEROL 101mg
IRON 1.7mg
SODIUM 309mg
CALCIUM 112mg

TIP: Cut whole skinless chicken breast halves into strips as a substitute for chicken tenders.

prep: 2 minutes ∞ **cook:** 35 minutes

Coriander Chicken ☑

Spice blends can become your secret ingredient in healthful cooking. One teaspoon of a robust, aromatic blend such as garam masala is enough to add big, bold flavor to chicken breasts and thighs and pork tenderloins or chops.

***POINTS* value: 5**

per serving:
CALORIES 230
FAT 7.4g (saturated fat 1.9g)
PROTEIN 37.7g
CARBOHYDRATE 0.7g
FIBER 0g
CHOLESTEROL 157mg
IRON 2.1mg
SODIUM 339mg
CALCIUM 22mg

TIP: Garam masala is an Indian blend of savory and sweet spices. Look for it on the spice aisle at your supermarket.

2 teaspoons dried coriander
1 teaspoon garam masala
½ teaspoon garlic salt
¼ teaspoon freshly ground black pepper
6 large chicken thighs (about 2 pounds), skinned
Cooking spray
1 cup fat-free, less-sodium chicken broth
1 tablespoon balsamic vinegar

1. Combine first 4 ingredients in a small bowl. Rub 1 side of chicken with spice mixture.

2. Heat a large nonstick skillet over medium-high heat; coat pan with cooking spray. Add chicken, and cook 4 minutes on each side or until browned. Add broth and vinegar to pan; cover and simmer 22 minutes or until chicken is done. Remove chicken from pan. Simmer sauce, uncovered, 5 minutes or until thick. Spoon sauce over chicken, and serve. Yield: 6 servings (serving size: 1 chicken thigh and about 2 teaspoons sauce).

prep: 25 minutes ∞ **cook:** 7 minutes ∞ **other:** 30 minutes

Pesto and Roasted Pepper Fish Kebabs

Prepare the kebabs ahead when you have extra time and refrigerate them. Then you'll only need to toss a salad while the kebabs cook on the grill. If you want to cook the vegetables longer without overcooking the fish, thread the fish and vegetables on separate skewers.

- 8 (12-inch) wooden skewers
- 1 green bell pepper, cut into 2-inch pieces
- 1 red bell pepper, cut into 2-inch pieces
- 1 yellow bell pepper, cut into 2-inch pieces
- 1 large red onion, cut into chunks
- 1½ pounds skinless halibut fillets, cut into 2-inch pieces
- ½ teaspoon salt
- ¼ teaspoon freshly ground black pepper
- 3 tablespoons prepared pesto (such as Buitoni)
- 2 teaspoons water
- Cooking spray
- Lemon wedges (optional)

1. Soak skewers in water 30 minutes.

2. Prepare grill.

3. Thread 2 pieces of bell pepper, 1 onion chunk, and 1 piece of fish alternately onto each skewer. Repeat this process 2 more times on each skewer, beginning and ending with bell pepper.

4. Sprinkle kebabs with salt and black pepper. Combine pesto and water; stir well. Brush kebabs evenly with half of pesto mixture.

5. Place skewers on grill rack coated with cooking spray. Grill 7 minutes, turning once halfway through to brush kebabs with remaining pesto. Serve with lemon wedges, if desired. Yield: 4 servings (serving size: 2 kebabs).

***POINTS* value: 6**

per serving:
CALORIES 283
FAT 9.5g (saturated fat 2g)
PROTEIN 38.7g
CARBOHYDRATE 9.7g
FIBER 2.3g
CHOLESTEROL 58mg
IRON 2.3mg
SODIUM 475mg
CALCIUM 180mg

TIP: Look for a trio of prepackaged bell peppers, usually red, green, and yellow, in the produce section of your supermarket. Generally, the package is less expensive than buying the peppers individually.

prep: 3 minutes ∞ **cook:** 12 minutes

Asian-Style Halibut

A few flavorful ingredients—soy sauce, sesame oil, and green onions—are all this quick recipe needs to deliver a delicious sauce for halibut steaks. Serve with ½ cup of brown rice and snow peas for a meal with a *POINTS* value of 7.

***POINTS* value: 5**

per serving:
CALORIES 222
FAT 6.7g (saturated fat 0.8g)
PROTEIN 36.6g
CARBOHYDRATE 2.4g
FIBER 0.6g
CHOLESTEROL 54mg
IRON 1.9mg
SODIUM 339mg
CALCIUM 99mg

TIP: Sesame oil has a nutty aroma and is excellent for everything from salad dressings to sautéing. It is commonly used as a flavoring ingredient in Asian dishes and can be found in the Asian section of your supermarket.

1½ teaspoons sesame oil
4 (6-ounce) halibut steaks (about 1 inch thick)
¼ teaspoon salt
⅛ teaspoon freshly ground black pepper
1 tablespoon low-sodium soy sauce, divided
6 green onions, cut into 2-inch julienne strips
1 tablespoon sesame seeds

1. Heat oil in a large nonstick skillet over medium-high heat. Sprinkle fish with salt and pepper. Add fish to pan; cook 5 minutes on each side or until fish flakes easily when tested with a fork.

2. Drizzle 1½ teaspoons soy sauce over fish. Remove fish from pan, and keep warm.

3. Add onions and sesame seeds to pan; cook 1 minute or until onions wilt. Drizzle remaining 1½ teaspoons soy sauce over onion mixture. Spoon onion mixture over fish, and serve. Yield: 4 servings (serving size: 1 halibut steak and one-fourth of onion mixture).

prep: 3 minutes ∞ **cook:** 15 minutes

Curried Salmon Steaks with Wilted Spinach ☑

Fresh baby spinach combined with a few savory spices are all you need to turn salmon into this appetizing Indian-inspired Core Plan® dish.

1¼ teaspoons curry powder
½ teaspoon salt, divided
¼ teaspoon freshly ground black pepper
¼ teaspoon garam masala
4 (6-ounce) salmon steaks (about 1 inch thick)
1 teaspoon olive oil, divided
Cooking spray
2 (6-ounce) packages fresh baby spinach

1. Combine curry powder, ¼ teaspoon salt, pepper, and garam marsala in a small bowl; sprinkle evenly over fish.

2. Heat ½ teaspoon oil in a large nonstick skillet over medium-high heat. Add fish, and cook 5 minutes on each side or until fish flakes easily when tested with a fork. Remove fish from pan; keep warm.

3. Coat pan with cooking spray; add remaining ½ teaspoon oil to pan, and place over medium heat. Add spinach, and cook 3 minutes or until spinach wilts. Sprinkle with remaining ¼ teaspoon salt.

4. Serve fish over spinach. Yield: 4 servings (serving size: 1 salmon steak and ¼ cup spinach).

***POINTS* value: 5**

per serving:
CALORIES 245
FAT 7.1g (saturated fat 1.1g)
PROTEIN 36g
CARBOHYDRATE 9.5g
FIBER 4.2g
CHOLESTEROL 88mg
IRON 4.2mg
SODIUM 540mg
CALCIUM 86mg

TIP: Don't be surprised by the amount of loose spinach. It wilts quickly, making room for all of the spinach to fit in the skillet.

prep: 13 minutes ∞ cook: 6 minutes

Salmon with Mango Salsa ☑

pictured on page 125

The fresh flavors of the salsa and salmon earned this recipe a high Test Kitchens rating. It can be prepared in 20 minutes, making it perfect for weeknight fare, but it's also special enough to serve to company.

***POINTS* value: 5**

per serving:
CALORIES 236
FAT 6.1g (saturated fat 1g)
PROTEIN 34g
CARBOHYDRATE 9.4g
FIBER 0.6g
CHOLESTEROL 88mg
IRON 1.3mg
SODIUM 405mg
CALCIUM 25mg

1 large mango, seeded and cubed
2 tablespoons minced red onion
1 tablespoon finely chopped fresh cilantro
1 tablespoon fresh lime juice
4 (6-ounce) salmon fillets (about 1 inch thick)
Cooking spray
½ teaspoon salt
¼ teaspoon freshly ground black pepper

1. Preheat broiler.

2. Place mango in a small bowl. Add next 3 ingredients, tossing well.

3. Place fish in a broiler pan coated with cooking spray; sprinkle fish with salt and pepper.

4. Broil 6 to 8 minutes or until fish flakes easily when tested with a fork. Serve salsa over fish. Yield: 4 servings (serving size: 1 fillet and ¼ cup salsa).

1. Hold the mango vertically on a cutting board. With a sharp knife, slice the fruit lengthwise on each side of the flat pit.

2. Holding a mango half in the palm of your hand, score the pulp in square cross-sections. Be sure that you slice to, but not through, the skin.

3. Turn the mango half inside out, and cut the chunks from the skin.

prep: 6 minutes ∞ **cook:** 8 minutes ∞ **other:** 5 minutes

Grilled Swordfish Steaks with Sun-Dried Tomato Butter

The sun-dried tomato butter adds zest and richness to this lean white fish. If you can't find swordfish, substitute grouper, halibut, or shark.

1 tablespoon sun-dried tomato sprinkles
1 tablespoon hot water
1/4 cup light stick butter, softened
1 tablespoon minced shallots
1 tablespoon minced fresh flat-leaf parsley
1/2 teaspoon bottled minced garlic
1/2 teaspoon salt, divided
1/2 teaspoon freshly ground black pepper, divided
4 (6-ounce) swordfish steaks (about 1 inch thick)
Olive oil–flavored cooking spray

1. Prepare grill.

2. Combine tomato sprinkles with 1 tablespoon hot water; let stand 5 minutes. Drain well. Combine sun-dried tomato, butter, and next 3 ingredients in a small bowl. Stir in 1/4 teaspoon each salt and pepper.

3. Coat fish lightly with cooking spray; sprinkle with remaining 1/4 teaspoon salt and remaining 1/4 teaspoon pepper. Grill 4 minutes on each side or until fish flakes easily when tested with a fork. Serve with a dollop of butter. Yield: 4 servings (serving size: 1 steak and 1 tablespoon butter).

***POINTS* value: 6**

per serving:
CALORIES 252
FAT 12.5g (saturated fat 5.3g)
PROTEIN 31.9g
CARBOHYDRATE 2.8g
FIBER 0.4g
CHOLESTEROL 77mg
IRON 1.5mg
SODIUM 540mg
CALCIUM 11mg

TIP: If you can't find sun-dried tomato sprinkles, mince whole sun-dried tomatoes instead.

prep: 9 minutes ∞ **cook:** 15 minutes

Swordfish with Lemon-Thyme Butter

Swordfish steaks are delectable when infused with lemon-thyme butter. The foil packet makes for easier cleanup.

***POINTS* value: 5**

per serving:
CALORIES 222
FAT 8.3g (saturated fat 2.7g)
PROTEIN 33.7g
CARBOHYDRATE 1.3g
FIBER 0.3g
CHOLESTEROL 70mg
IRON 1.5mg
SODIUM 323mg
CALCIUM 13mg

TIP: One lemon will yield the rind, juice, and slices for this recipe. Grate the rind before slicing the lemon in half.

1 teaspoon grated fresh lemon rind
1 teaspoon fresh lemon juice
1 tablespoon light stick butter, softened
Cooking spray
4 (6-ounce) swordfish steaks (about 1¼ inches thick)
¼ teaspoon salt
¼ teaspoon freshly ground black pepper
1 tablespoon chopped fresh thyme
8 thin lemon slices (½ lemon)

1. Preheat oven to 425°.

2. Stir together first 3 ingredients a small bowl. Set aside.

3. Cut 2 (18 x 12–inch) rectangles of foil. Spray 1 sheet of foil with cooking spray; place fish in center of sheet. Sprinkle fish with salt, pepper, and thyme.

4. Top fish evenly with butter mixture. Layer lemon slices over fish. Cover fish with other sheet of foil, and fold edges together to form a tight seal. Place foil packet on a baking sheet.

5. Bake at 425° for 15 to 17 minutes or until fish flakes easily when tested with a fork. Remove fish from foil, and transfer to plates. Serve immediately. Yield: 4 servings (serving size: 1 swordfish steak and 2 lemon slices).

prep: 5 minutes ∞ **cook:** 5 minutes

Seared Sea Scallops with Chipotle Aïoli

Aïoli is a strongly flavored mayonnaise that's typically made with garlic and served with fish, meats, or vegetables. We've created a smoky and spicy version that pairs well with seared scallops. Serve this superquick entrée with steamed broccoli and ½ cup of boiled red potatoes for a meal with a *POINTS* value of 8.

- ½ cup light mayonnaise
- 1½ tablespoons fresh lime juice
- 1 teaspoon adobo sauce from canned chipotle peppers in adobo sauce
- 1½ pounds sea scallops (about 40)
- 2 teaspoons olive oil
- ¼ teaspoon salt
- ⅛ teaspoon black pepper

1. Stir together first 3 ingredients in a small bowl; set aside.

2. Rinse and drain scallops. Pat scallops dry with paper towels to remove excess moisture.

3. Heat a large nonstick skillet over medium-high heat 1 to 2 minutes or until hot; add oil. Add scallops, and sprinkle with salt and pepper. Cook scallops 2 minutes; turn and cook 2 to 3 minutes or until golden brown. Transfer to a serving platter. Serve with Chipotle Aïoli. Yield: 4 servings (serving size: about 10 scallops and 2 tablespoons aïoli).

***POINTS* value: 7**

per serving:
CALORIES 272
FAT 13.5g (saturated fat 2g)
PROTEIN 28.8g
CARBOHYDRATE 7.2g
FIBER 0.2g
CHOLESTEROL 67mg
IRON 0.6mg
SODIUM 672mg
CALCIUM 44mg

TIP: To get the best sear on scallops, pat the scallops with paper towels to make sure they are very dry. Preheat the skillet until it's hot, and then quickly add a few of the scallops at a time to the skillet and wait for them to sizzle before adding more. Don't crowd the skillet. If necessary, cook in two batches. Cook on one side for a full two minutes before turning.

prep: 6 minutes ∞ **cook:** 3 minutes ∞ **other:** 30 minutes

Mango Shrimp Kebabs

Not only will you enjoy the sweet and tangy flavors of mango and lime, but you'll also be pleased that this dish can be prepped and cooked with very little effort. We used jarred mango to keep the prep time low, but substitute fresh mango if you wish.

***POINTS* value: 6**

per serving:
CALORIES 304
FAT 2.2g (saturated fat 0.5g)
PROTEIN 31.8g
CARBOHYDRATE 38.1g
FIBER 0.9g
CHOLESTEROL 294mg
IRON 5mg
SODIUM 647mg
CALCIUM 69mg

TIP: To save prep time, instead of peeling and deveining your own shrimp, ask someone in the seafood market to peel and devein them for you. It might cost a little extra, but it's worth it if you're in a hurry.

8 (12-inch) wooden skewers
40 medium shrimp, peeled and deveined (about 1¾ pounds)
½ (24-ounce) jar mango slices in light syrup (about 7 slices)
5½ tablespoons mango chutney, divided
2 tablespoons lime juice, divided
½ teaspoon grated fresh lime rind, divided
½ teaspoon dark sesame oil, divided
⅛ teaspoon salt

1. Soak skewers in water 30 minutes.

2. Prepare grill.

3. Thread 5 shrimp onto each skewer. Set aside.

4. Place mango slices, 1½ tablespoons chutney, 1 tablespoon lime juice, ¼ teaspoon lime rind, ¼ teaspoon sesame oil, and salt in a food processor; process until smooth, stopping to scrape down sides. Transfer to a small bowl; set aside.

5. Stir together remaining 4 tablespoons chutney, remaining 1 tablespoon lime juice, and remaining ¼ teaspoon each of lime rind and sesame oil. Brush chutney mixture over both sides of shrimp. Grill 1½ to 2 minutes on each side or until shrimp are done, basting with chutney mixture. Serve with reserved mango sauce. Yield: 4 servings (serving size: 2 kebabs and 2 tablespoons sauce).

prep: 7 minutes ∞ **cook:** 50 minutes ∞ **other:** 10 minutes

Barbecue Meat Loaf

Use your family's favorite barbecue sauce for this popular stick-to-your ribs dish. Whether you prefer a sweet, smoky, or tangy sauce, it will be a delicious addition to this low-fat meat loaf that we kept juicy and tender by combining egg whites, minced onion, and ground round.

- 2/3 cup barbecue sauce, divided
- 1/4 cup minced onion
- 1 tablespoon Worcestershire sauce
- 1/2 teaspoon salt
- 1/4 teaspoon black pepper
- 2 large egg whites
- 1 1/2 pounds ground round
- 1/2 cup quick-cooking oats
- Cooking spray

1. Preheat oven to 350°.

2. Combine 1/3 cup barbecue sauce and next 4 ingredients in a large bowl. Add egg whites, and crumble meat over mixture, mixing with hands just until blended; add oats, and stir until blended.

3. Shape meat mixture into an 8 x 4–inch loaf, and place on a broiler pan coated with cooking spray.

4. Bake at 350° for 30 minutes. Brush remaining 1/3 cup barbecue sauce over meat loaf. Bake an additional 20 minutes or until done. Let stand 10 minutes. Cut loaf into 12 slices. Yield: 6 servings (serving size: 2 slices).

***POINTS* value: 4**

per serving:
CALORIES 210
FAT 4.5g (saturated fat 1.6g)
PROTEIN 26.2g
CARBOHYDRATE 16.6g
FIBER 0.7g
CHOLESTEROL 60mg
IRON 2.3mg
SODIUM 688mg
CALCIUM 9mg

TIP: Use your hands to separate an egg instead of pouring the egg yolk back and forth from one half of the eggshell to the other (which increases the likelihood of the shell breaking the yolk and the chance of transferring bacteria). Just crack the egg and let the white run through your fingers into a bowl. Wash your hands before and after.

prep: 5 minutes ∞ **cook:** 20 minutes ∞ **other:** overnight and 15 minutes

Teriyaki Tri-Tip

Tri-tip, which gets its name from its triangular shape, may also be labeled as sirloin butt. When cutting this meat, you may have to rotate the meat several times to always cut against the grain.

***POINTS* value: 5**

per serving:
CALORIES 227
FAT 8.7g (saturated fat 3.2g)
PROTEIN 24.5g
CARBOHYDRATE 9.3g
FIBER 0g
CHOLESTEROL 66mg
IRON 2mg
SODIUM 458mg
CALCIUM 36mg

TIP: Mirin is a low-alcohol golden-hued rice wine that adds a subtle sweetness. It is commonly used in Asian cuisine and can be found in many large supermarkets.

¾ cup low-sodium soy sauce
½ cup thinly sliced onion
⅓ cup firmly packed brown sugar
⅓ cup mirin (sweet rice wine)
1 tablespoon thinly sliced fresh ginger
3 garlic cloves, crushed
½ teaspoon black pepper
1 (1½-pound) tri-tip roast
Cooking spray

1. Combine first 7 ingredients in a large zip-top plastic bag. Add roast; seal bag, and marinate roast in refrigerator overnight, turning bag occasionally.

2. Prepare grill.

3. Remove roast from bag; strain marinade, and reserve ½ cup. Discard solids. Place roast on grill rack coated with cooking spray; grill 10 minutes on each side or until desired degree of doneness. Let stand 15 minutes before slicing.

4. While roast stands, bring reserved marinade to a boil in a small saucepan; boil 2 minutes.

5. Cut roast diagonally across grain into thin slices; serve with warm marinade. Yield: 6 servings (serving size: 3 ounces beef and about 1 tablespoon marinade).

prep: 3 minutes ⚮ **cook:** 14 minutes

Pork Chops with Pineapple Salsa ☑

Boneless center-cut pork chops, like boneless chicken breasts, are a great convenience. They're lower in fat than other cuts of meat, and they adapt to a variety of quick cooking methods, including searing, grilling, and baking.

- ½ cup bottled chunky salsa
- 2 green onions, chopped
- 1 (8-ounce) can crushed pineapple in juice, undrained
- 1 tablespoon canola oil
- 4 (4-ounce) boneless center-cut loin pork chops (about ½ inch thick)

1. Combine first 3 ingredients in a bowl; set aside.

2. Heat oil in a large nonstick skillet over medium-high heat. Add chops to pan; cook 3 minutes on each side or until brown. Add salsa mixture to pan; simmer, uncovered, 8 minutes or until pork is done. Yield: 4 servings (serving size: 1 pork chop and ¼ cup salsa).

***POINTS* value: 5**

per serving:
CALORIES 237
FAT 10.1g (saturated fat 2.7g)
PROTEIN 23.8g
CARBOHYDRATE 12.8g
FIBER 0.8g
CHOLESTEROL 67mg
IRON 1.2mg
SODIUM 281mg
CALCIUM 35mg

TIP: Purchase extra boneless chops when they're on sale. Wrap each chop in plastic wrap, place in a heavy-duty zip-top freezer bag, and freeze. Thaw only the number of chops you need.

prep: 4 minutes ∞ **cook:** 11 minutes

Blueberry-Balsamic Pork Cutlets

pictured on page 42

When your family tastes these tender cutlets in a sweet blueberry-balsamic sauce, they'll never suspect you made dinner at the last minute.

***POINTS* value: 5**

per serving:
CALORIES 209
FAT 6.4g (saturated fat 2.3g)
PROTEIN 24g
CARBOHYDRATE 12g
FIBER 0.1g
CHOLESTEROL 65mg
IRON 0.8mg
SODIUM 196mg
CALCIUM 28mg

TIP: Pork cutlets are very thin, so they don't need to be pounded, and they cook quickly. Overcooking may cause the cutlets to be tough.

8 (2-ounce) boneless center-cut loin pork chops (¼ inch thick)
¼ teaspoon salt
¼ teaspoon black pepper
2 tablespoons balsamic vinegar
¼ cup blueberry spread (such as Polaner All Fruit)
Cooking spray
2 tablespoons chopped shallots
1 teaspoon fresh thyme

1. Sprinkle both sides of pork with salt and pepper. Combine vinegar and blueberry spread, stirring with a whisk. Set aside.

2. Heat a large nonstick skillet over medium-high heat; coat pan with cooking spray. Add half of pork, and cook 2 minutes on each side. Remove pork from pan; keep warm. Repeat procedure with remaining pork.

3. Add shallots to pan, and cook 30 seconds, stirring constantly. Add blueberry mixture to pan; cook 30 seconds, scraping pan to loosen browned bits. Return pork and any juices to pan. Cook 45 seconds; turn and cook 45 seconds or until pork is thoroughly heated. Sprinkle with thyme. Yield: 4 servings (serving size: 2 pork cutlets and 1 tablespoon sauce).

prep: 6 minutes ∞ **cook:** 4 minutes

Grilled Pork Medallions ☑

We've reduced the cooking time in this recipe by slicing the tenderloin into medallions. The fresh herbs and garlic paired with Dijon mustard add savory seasonings to this tender and juicy dish.

- 1 (1¼-pound) pork tenderloin, trimmed
- 1 tablespoon olive oil
- 1 tablespoon Dijon mustard
- 1 tablespoon minced fresh oregano
- 1½ teaspoons minced garlic
- 1 teaspoon freshly ground black pepper
- ½ teaspoon salt

1. Prepare grill.

2. Cut pork crosswise into ¼-inch-thick slices.

3. Combine olive oil and next 5 ingredients; rub over pork, coating well.

4. Grill pork 1 to 2 minutes on each side or until pork is done. Serve immediately. Yield: 5 servings (serving size: 3 ounces).

***POINTS* value: 4**

per serving:
CALORIES 171
FAT 7.1g (saturated fat 1.7g)
PROTEIN 24.1g
CARBOHYDRATE 1.2g
FIBER 0.2g
CHOLESTEROL 74mg
IRON 1.5mg
SODIUM 351mg
CALCIUM 13mg

TIP: Use long-handled tongs rather than a fork to quickly turn the pork on the grill.

prep: 2 minutes ∞ **cook:** 13 minutes

Szechuan Pork and Vegetables

Save prep time by using presliced vegetables in this tangy stir-fry. Look for packages of the veggies in your supermarket's produce department. We loved this simple stir-fry served over hot cooked rice.

***POINTS* value: 8**

per serving:
CALORIES 377
FAT 4g (saturated fat 1.4g)
PROTEIN 29.1g
CARBOHYDRATE 53.8g
FIBER 1.6g
CHOLESTEROL 74mg
IRON 3.2mg
SODIUM 465mg
CALCIUM 25mg

TIP: To make slicing the tenderloin easier, place the meat in the freezer for about 10 minutes so it can get slightly firm. Set a timer to remind you to take the meat out before it freezes.

2 (3.5-ounce) bags boil-in-bag rice
1 (1-pound) pork tenderloin, trimmed
1 tablespoon chili sauce (such as Hokan)
Cooking spray
4 cups presliced onion and red and green bell pepper strips
¾ cup less-sodium beef broth
¼ cup low-sodium teriyaki sauce
1 tablespoon cornstarch

1. Cook rice according to package directions, omitting salt and fat.

2. While rice cooks, cut pork in half lengthwise; cut crosswise into ¼-inch-thick slices. Toss pork with chili sauce.

3. Heat a large nonstick skillet over medium-high heat; coat pan with cooking spray. Add pork; sauté 3 minutes or until done. Remove from pan, and keep warm.

4. Add vegetables to pan. Cook 4 minutes or until vegetables are tender, stirring occasionally.

5. Combine broth, teriyaki sauce, and cornstarch in a small bowl. Return pork to pan; add cornstarch mixture, stirring well. Bring to a simmer over medium heat; cook 1 minute or until thick. Yield: 4 servings (serving size: about 1¼ cups pork mixture and ¾ cup rice).

prep: 8 minutes ∞ **cook:** 4 minutes

Pulled-Pork Sandwiches

pictured on page 46

With the help of a store-bought pork roast *au jus*, these fuss-free sandwiches can easily be ready in 12 minutes.

1 (17-ounce) package precooked pork roast au jus
2½ cups preshredded cabbage
½ cup light sweet Vidalia onion dressing (such as Ken's Steak House)
¾ teaspoon ground cumin
6 (1.6-ounce) whole wheat hamburger buns
Pickle slices (optional)

1. Heat pork according to package directions.

2. Meanwhile, combine cabbage and dressing; set aside.

3. Transfer pork to a medium bowl, reserving ¼ cup juices. Remove and discard any fat from pork. Shred pork with 2 forks. Stir in reserved juices and cumin.

4. Spoon ⅓ cup pork onto bottom halves of buns. Spoon ¼ cup slaw mixture over pork on each bun. Top with pickle slices, if desired. Cover with top halves of buns. Yield: 6 servings (serving size: 1 sandwich).

***POINTS* value: 6**

per serving:
CALORIES 279
FAT 9.1g (saturated fat 2.1g)
PROTEIN 20.3g
CARBOHYDRATE 31.6g
FIBER 4g
CHOLESTEROL 49mg
IRON 2.1mg
SODIUM 636mg
CALCIUM 75mg

TIP: If you prefer your meat sliced rather than shredded, place the meat on a cutting board and use a sharp knife to cut the meat into thin slices.

prep: 8 minutes ∞ **cook:** 12 minutes

BLTs with Pimiento Cheese

pictured on back cover

Just when you thought nothing was better than crisp bacon combined with a ripe, juicy tomato, try sandwiching it between layers of pimiento cheese.

***POINTS* value: 6**

per serving:
CALORIES 272
FAT 9.7g (saturated fat 3.5g)
PROTEIN 15.7g
CARBOHYDRATE 29.2g
FIBER 3g
CHOLESTEROL 25mg
IRON 2.5mg
SODIUM 968mg
CALCIUM 127mg

TIP: If you prefer to bake the bacon for this recipe, line a rimmed baking sheet with parchment paper. Lay the bacon strips on the paper, being careful not to overlap the bacon. Bake at 400° for 15 to 18 minutes or until the bacon is crisp and brown. Rotate the pan once during baking. Drain on paper towels.

- ½ cup light pimiento cheese spread (such as Price's)
- 8 (1-ounce) slices whole wheat bread
- 12 reduced-fat bacon slices, cooked
- 4 green leaf lettuce leaves
- 12 (¼-inch-thick) slices tomato (about 3 tomatoes)
- ⅛ teaspoon salt
- ¼ teaspoon freshly ground black pepper

1. Spread 1 tablespoon pimiento cheese over each bread slice.

2. Top each of 4 bread slices with 3 bacon slices, 1 lettuce leaf, and 3 tomato slices.

3. Sprinkle evenly with salt and pepper. Cover with remaining 4 bread slices. Cut each sandwich in half, and secure with wooden picks, if desired. Yield: 4 servings (serving size: 1 sandwich).

prep: 12 minutes ∞ **cook:** 8 minutes ∞ **other:** 12 minutes

Grilled Tofu with Sesame-Ginger Marinade

The bold combination of brown sugar, soy sauce, garlic, and ginger gives a sweet and savory touch to tofu that's allowed to marinate two to three minutes after grilling.

- 1 (16-ounce) package water-packed firm tofu
- 1/4 teaspoon salt
- 2 tablespoons brown sugar
- 1 tablespoon sesame seeds
- 1/2 teaspoon ground ginger
- 1/4 teaspoon garlic powder
- 3 tablespoons low-sodium soy sauce
- 1/2 teaspoon hot pepper sauce (such as Tabasco)
- 1 tablespoon finely chopped fresh cilantro

1. Drain tofu, and cut lengthwise into 6 slices. Place slices on several layers of heavy-duty paper towels. Cover tofu with additional paper towels; let stand 10 minutes.

2. Prepare grill or indoor grill pan.

3. Sprinkle tofu with salt. Grill 4 to 6 minutes or until grill marks appear. Turn tofu and grill on other side for 4 to 6 minutes. Place 2 slices tofu, in a single layer, on each of 3 plates.

4. Combine brown sugar and next 5 ingredients in a small bowl; stir until well blended. Spoon about 2 teaspoons soy sauce mixture over each serving; sprinkle with cilantro, and let stand 2 to 3 minutes. Yield: 3 servings (serving size: 2 slices tofu).

***POINTS* value: 5**

per serving:
CALORIES 197
FAT 11.3g (saturated fat 1.7g)
PROTEIN 18.4g
CARBOHYDRATE 9.5g
FIBER 1.7g
CHOLESTEROL 0mg
IRON 3.5mg
SODIUM 607mg
CALCIUM 178mg

TIP: Drain the tofu slices between several layers of paper towels to absorb the extra moisture so that the tofu will brown quickly on the grill.

prep: 4 minutes ∞ **cook:** 6 minutes ∞ **other:** 1 hour

Open-Faced Black Bean Burgers

For a meatless meal, serve these burgers with ½ cup of crunchy raw veggies, such as cucumbers, celery, or baby carrots, and 1 tablespoon of reduced-fat ranch or blue cheese dressing for a meal with a *POINTS* value of 8. You can top the burgers with 1 tablespoon of guacamole for an additional *POINTS* value of 1.

***POINTS* value: 7**

per serving:
CALORIES 331
FAT 8.6g (saturated fat 1.6g)
PROTEIN 12.1g
CARBOHYDRATE 54.1g
FIBER 7.6g
CHOLESTEROL 106mg
IRON 3mg
SODIUM 742mg
CALCIUM 100mg

TIP: The next time you cook brown rice, plan ahead and make enough rice so you'll have enough left over for this recipe.

- 1 (15-ounce) can 50%-less-sodium black beans (such as S&W), rinsed and drained
- ¾ cup cooked instant brown rice
- ½ cup Italian-seasoned breadcrumbs
- 2 large eggs, lightly beaten
- ½ teaspoon garlic salt
- ½ teaspoon freshly ground black pepper
- 1 tablespoon olive oil
- 2 (1.6-ounce) whole wheat hamburger buns
- 1 cup shredded lettuce
- ¼ cup refrigerated fresh salsa
- Reduced-fat sour cream (optional)

1. Place beans in a medium bowl; mash slightly with a fork or potato masher, leaving some beans whole.

2. Stir in rice and next 4 ingredients. Cover and chill at least 1 hour.

3. Divide bean mixture into 4 equal portions; shape each portion into a 1-inch-thick patty.

4. Heat oil in a large nonstick skillet over medium-high heat. Add patties, and cook 4 minutes or until browned. Turn patties and cook 2 to 3 minutes or until browned and thoroughly heated.

5. Place 1 patty on each bun half; top evenly with lettuce and salsa. Place a dollop of sour cream on top of salsa, if desired. Serve immediately. Yield: 4 servings (serving size: 1 open-faced burger).

One-Dish Meals

prep: 16 minutes ∞ **cook:** 53 minutes ∞ **other:** 10 minutes

Creamy Chicken-Rice Casserole

This savory and comforting casserole has a nostalgic appeal. Its buttery, crunchy topping and creamy center will surely please any picky eater.

***POINTS* value: 8**

per serving:
CALORIES 329
FAT 15.5g (saturated fat 4.9g)
PROTEIN 20.6g
CARBOHYDRATE 24.9g
FIBER 1.6g
CHOLESTEROL 59mg
IRON 1.9mg
SODIUM 539mg
CALCIUM 175mg

TIP: Thaw the broccoli in the microwave at HIGH for two minutes.

1½ cups fat-free milk
2½ tablespoons all-purpose flour
¼ teaspoon salt
¼ teaspoon black pepper
1 cup (4 ounces) reduced-fat shredded sharp Cheddar cheese
⅓ cup ⅓-less-fat cream cheese
3 cups chopped cooked chicken breast
1 cup light mayonnaise
¾ cup chopped onion
1 (8-ounce) can diced water chestnuts, drained
1 (10-ounce) package frozen chopped broccoli, thawed and drained
1¾ cups cooked rice
Cooking spray
35 reduced-fat round buttery crackers (about 1 sleeve; such as Ritz), crushed

1. Preheat oven to 375°.

2. Combine milk and next 3 ingredients in a large saucepan over medium-high heat, stirring with a whisk; bring to a boil. Cook 1 minute or until thick, stirring constantly. Remove from heat, and add cheeses, stirring until smooth. Combine cheese sauce with chicken and next 5 ingredients in a large bowl. Spoon chicken mixture into a 13 x 9–inch baking dish coated with cooking spray.

3. Sprinkle crushed crackers on top of chicken mixture; spray crackers with cooking spray. Bake at 375° for 30 to 40 minutes or until casserole is bubbly and crackers are golden brown. Let stand 10 minutes before serving. Yield: 10 servings (serving size: 1 cup).

prep: 2 minutes ∞ **cook:** 1 hour and 15 minutes ∞ **other:** 5 minutes

Chicken Tetrazzini

This rich pasta-and-chicken dish is topped with Parmesan cheese and baked until it's bubbly and golden.

12 ounces uncooked spaghetti
2 tablespoons light stick butter
1 (8-ounce) package presliced mushrooms
3 cups chopped cooked chicken breast
2 (10.75-ounce) cans condensed 45% reduced-sodium, 98% fat-free cream of mushroom soup (such as Campbell's Healthy Request), undiluted
2 cups reduced-fat sour cream
½ teaspoon freshly ground black pepper
Cooking spray
⅓ cup grated Parmesan cheese

1. Preheat oven to 350°.

2. Cook spaghetti according to package directions, omitting salt and fat. Drain.

3. While pasta cooks, melt butter in a nonstick skillet over medium-high heat. Add mushrooms, and sauté 4 minutes or until tender.

4. Combine pasta, mushrooms, chicken, and next 3 ingredients.

5. Pour chicken mixture into a 13 x 9–inch baking dish coated with cooking spray. Sprinkle with Parmesan cheese. Bake at 350° for 55 minutes or until bubbly. Let stand 5 minutes before serving. Yield: 9 servings (serving size: 1 cup).

***POINTS* value: 8**

per serving:
CALORIES 370
FAT 12.5g (saturated fat 6.6g)
PROTEIN 24g
CARBOHYDRATE 38.6g
FIBER 1.9g
CHOLESTEROL 76mg
IRON 2mg
SODIUM 392mg
CALCIUM 193mg

TIP: Presliced produce, such as the mushrooms we call for in this recipe, can be a lifesaver when you want to use fresh fruits and vegetables but are short on time. Just make sure that the produce looks fresh in the package.

prep: 10 minutes ∞ **cook:** 25 minutes

Black Bean–Chicken Enchilada Casserole

Instead of being rolled like most enchiladas, this tasty Tex-Mex dish is layered, resulting in a prep time of 10 minutes.

***POINTS* value: 8**

per serving:
CALORIES 402
FAT 12.6g (saturated fat 6g)
PROTEIN 38g
CARBOHYDRATE 36.4g
FIBER 7.5g
CHOLESTEROL 88mg
IRON 2.8mg
SODIUM 534mg
CALCIUM 379mg

TIP: Cumin is a savory spice that's widely used in Mexican and Indian cuisines as well as Mediterranean and North African dishes. To preserve its potency, store it in a cool, dark place or in your freezer.

- 3 (8-ounce) cans no-salt-added tomato sauce
- ½ cup salsa
- 1 teaspoon ground cumin
- 3 cups chopped cooked chicken breast
- 1 (15-ounce) can black beans, rinsed and drained
- 1 (4.5-ounce) can chopped green chiles, undrained
- 12 (5-inch) corn tortillas
- 1 cup (4 ounces) reduced-fat shredded sharp Cheddar cheese
- 1 cup (4 ounces) reduced-fat shredded Monterey Jack cheese
- ¾ cup reduced-fat sour cream (optional)
- ½ cup chopped green onions (optional)

1. Preheat oven to 350°.

2. Combine first 3 ingredients; stir well. Spread ¾ cup tomato sauce mixture in bottom of a 13 x 9–inch baking dish. Set aside.

3. Combine chicken, black beans, green chiles, and ½ cup tomato sauce mixture in a medium bowl. Stir well.

4. Place 6 tortillas on top of tomato sauce mixture in baking dish; top with half of chicken mixture and half of remaining tomato sauce mixture. Repeat layers with remaining tortillas, chicken mixture, and tomato sauce mixture. Sprinkle with cheeses. Bake at 350° for 25 minutes. Top with sour cream and onions, if desired. Cut into 6 equal portions. Yield: 6 servings (serving size: 1 [4 x 4½–inch] rectangle).

Raisin Brownie Bars, page 188

Soft Taco,
page 50

Tamale Pie,
page 140

Asparagus with Balsamic Butter, page 158

Rosemary-Orange Pork Roast with Acorn Squash and Sweet Potatoes, page 82

Southwestern Chicken Pizza, page 52

Caramelized Peaches with Vanilla Frozen Yogurt, page 179

Couscous and Chicken Salad, page 60

Cornmeal-Crusted Chicken Fingers, page 88

Roast Beef Wraps, page 17

Italian Sausage with Peppers and Tomatoes, page 134

Individual Apple-Blueberry Crumble, page 175

Chicken Quesadillas,
page 25

Skillet Lasagna, page 138

prep: 3 minutes ∞ **cook:** 24 minutes

Quick Chicken Cacciatore

While bone-in chicken breasts take a little longer to cook than boneless breasts, the resulting flavor is worth the extra time. Searing the chicken and then simmering it in a robust sauce creates a high-flavor meal that can be ready to eat in about 30 minutes.

Cooking spray
3 cups thinly sliced onion (about 1 pound)
4 (8-ounce) bone-in chicken breast halves, skinned
¼ teaspoon freshly ground black pepper
1 (26-ounce) jar fire-roasted tomato and garlic pasta sauce (such as Classico)
½ cup sliced green olives
⅓ cup chopped fresh parsley
4 ounces uncooked vermicelli

1. Heat a large Dutch oven coated with cooking spray over medium-high heat. Add onion, and sauté 4 minutes or until onion begins to brown; move onion to 1 side of pan.

2. Sprinkle chicken with pepper; add to pan, and cook 2 minutes on each side or until browned. Add pasta sauce and olives, and reduce heat to medium-low. Simmer, covered, for 16 minutes or until chicken is done. Stir in parsley.

3. While chicken simmers, cook pasta according to package directions, omitting salt and fat.

4. Drain pasta. Serve chicken and sauce over pasta. Yield: 4 servings (serving size: 1 chicken breast half, about ⅔ cup sauce, and about ½ cup pasta).

***POINTS* value: 7**

per serving:
CALORIES 444
FAT 5.1g (saturated fat 1g)
PROTEIN 50.2g
CARBOHYDRATE 48.8g
FIBER 5.9g
CHOLESTEROL 105mg
IRON 4.6mg
SODIUM 894mg
CALCIUM 126mg

TIP: Water will come to a boil faster with the lid on the pot. However, after the pasta is added to the water, don't replace the lid. Bring the water back to a boil, and cook, uncovered, until the pasta is done, stirring occasionally.

prep: 22 minutes ∞ **cook:** 42 minutes

Chicken Fricassee

A fricassee is a thick, chunky stew. It's the ultimate comfort food—a creamy dish of succulent chicken and tender vegetables smothered in a rich brown gravy. For a delightful variation, serve over mashed potatoes or grits.

***POINTS* value: 7**

per serving:
CALORIES 392
FAT 4.8g (saturated fat 1.9g)
PROTEIN 46.6g
CARBOHYDRATE 38.6g
FIBER 3.7g
CHOLESTEROL 110mg
IRON 3.8mg
SODIUM 623mg
CALCIUM 78mg

TIP: Freeze any leftover chicken broth in ½-cup muffin cups to keep on hand for future use. Remove the frozen broth from the cups; place the broth in freezer bags for up to two months. Be sure to write on the freezer bag that each cube of frozen broth equals ½ cup.

3 tablespoons all-purpose flour
1 teaspoon paprika
½ teaspoon poultry seasoning
½ teaspoon black pepper
4 (8-ounce) bone-in chicken breast halves, skinned
½ teaspoon salt
2 teaspoons butter
1½ cups chopped onion (about 1 medium)
½ cup chopped celery
3 garlic cloves, minced
1 cup fat-free, less-sodium chicken broth
2 cups matchstick-cut carrots
¼ cup chopped fresh parsley
2 cups hot cooked rice

1. Combine first 4 ingredients in a large zip-top plastic bag. Add chicken; toss well to coat. Remove chicken from bag; reserve flour mixture. Sprinkle chicken with salt.

2. Melt butter in a large nonstick skillet over medium heat. Add chicken, breast sides down, and cook 4 to 5 minutes or until chicken is browned. Remove chicken from pan; keep warm.

3. Add onion, celery, and garlic to pan; sauté 7 minutes, stirring often. Stir in reserved flour mixture, and cook 1 minute, stirring occasionally. Add broth; bring to a boil. Stir in carrots. Return chicken to pan, breast sides up. Cover, reduce heat, and simmer 25 minutes or until chicken is done. Sprinkle with chopped parsley. Serve over rice. Yield: 4 servings (serving size: 1 chicken breast half, about ½ cup sauce, and ½ cup rice).

prep: 2 minutes ∞ **cook:** 40 minutes

Tuscan Chicken Soup

Here's a mouthwatering chicken soup that is almost too good to be true—two minutes of preparation time and one pot for cooking.

Cooking spray
2 garlic cloves, minced
½ cup chopped onion
1 pound ground chicken breast
2 (14-ounce) cans fat-free, less-sodium chicken broth
½ cup uncooked orzo (rice-shaped pasta)
1 (14.5-ounce) can stewed tomatoes, undrained and chopped
1 (16-ounce) can chickpeas (garbanzo beans), rinsed and drained
1 teaspoon dried basil
1 teaspoon dried oregano
¼ teaspoon freshly ground black pepper
1 (6-ounce) package fresh baby spinach
6 teaspoons shredded Parmesan cheese

1. Heat a large saucepan over medium heat; coat pan with cooking spray. Add garlic and onion; sauté 5 minutes or until just tender. Add chicken, and cook 5 minutes, stirring to crumble.

2. Add broth and next 6 ingredients. Bring to a boil; reduce heat, and simmer 22 minutes or until orzo is done.

3. Stir in spinach; cook 3 minutes or until spinach wilts. Ladle soup into bowls; top with cheese. Yield: 6 servings (serving size: 1½ cups soup and 1 teaspoon cheese).

***POINTS* value: 4**

per serving:
CALORIES 216
FAT 2g (saturated fat 0.8g)
PROTEIN 23.9g
CARBOHYDRATE 25.5g
FIBER 4.5g
CHOLESTEROL 45mg
IRON 2.7mg
SODIUM 694mg
CALCIUM 98mg

TIP: Save both prep and cleanup time by using kitchen shears to chop the tomatoes right in the can.

prep: 3 minutes ∞ cook: 21 minutes

Turkey and Tomatillo Chili

Simmer a pot of chili for dinner tonight and you just might have enough left over for lunch tomorrow. You can make it mild or spicy, depending on your choice of salsa.

***POINTS* value: 3**

per serving:
CALORIES 160
FAT 2.8g (saturated fat 1.2g)
PROTEIN 22.6g
CARBOHYDRATE 13.4g
FIBER 3.7g
CHOLESTEROL 30mg
IRON 1.5mg
SODIUM 635mg
CALCIUM 34mg

TIP: Green salsa is made from tomatillos and green chiles. Look for it near the regular salsas in the Mexican or Latin food section of your grocery store.

Cooking spray
1½ pounds ground turkey breast
1 cup chopped onion
2 (15.8-ounce) cans Great Northern beans, rinsed and drained
1 (16-ounce) bottle green salsa
1 (14-ounce) can fat-free, less-sodium chicken broth
1½ teaspoons ground cumin
2 tablespoons coarsely chopped fresh cilantro
½ cup low-fat sour cream
Cilantro sprigs

1. Heat a Dutch oven over medium heat; coat pan with cooking spray. Add turkey and onion, and cook until turkey is browned and onion is tender, stirring to crumble turkey.

2. Stir in beans and next 3 ingredients; bring to a boil. Reduce heat to medium, and simmer 5 minutes.

3. Stir in chopped cilantro. Ladle soup into bowls; top with sour cream and cilantro sprigs. Yield: 9 servings (serving size: 1 cup soup and about 1 tablespoon sour cream).

prep: 8 minutes ∞ cook: 9 minutes

Creamy Potato and Sausage Soup

Frozen mashed potatoes shave minutes off the prep time for this soup. Serve this savory soup with a garden salad and a piece of crusty bread.

Cooking spray
4 ounces chopped smoked turkey sausage (such as Healthy Choice)
1 cup chopped green onions (about 4)
2 cups 1% low-fat milk
1 (14-ounce) can fat-free, less-sodium chicken broth
4 cups frozen mashed potatoes (such as Ore-Ida)
1 teaspoon dried thyme
¼ teaspoon black pepper
⅛ teaspoon salt

1. Heat a medium saucepan over medium-high heat; coat pan with cooking spray. Add sausage and onions; sauté 4 minutes or until onions are tender.

2. Add milk and remaining ingredients. Cook over medium heat 5 minutes or until thoroughly heated, stirring constantly with a whisk. Serve immediately. Yield: 4 servings (serving size: 1¼ cups).

***POINTS* value: 5**

per serving:
CALORIES 244
FAT 5.6g (saturated fat 2.8g)
PROTEIN 10.4g
CARBOHYDRATE 35.6g
FIBER 2.7g
CHOLESTEROL 18mg
IRON 0.9mg
SODIUM 862mg
CALCIUM 177mg

TIP: Trim the top third and the root ends from the green onions. Gather them together, aligning the cut root ends, and place on a cutting board. Use a chef's knife to quickly chop the onions.

prep: 6 minutes ∞ **cook:** 14 minutes

Italian Sausage with Peppers and Tomatoes

pictured on page 123

Dinner doesn't get much easier than this 20-minute meal. The chunky sauce comes together in the same amount of time it takes to cook the pasta, so put the pot of water on to boil before beginning the recipe.

***POINTS* value: 6**

per serving:
CALORIES 280
FAT 6.8g (saturated fat 0.2g)
PROTEIN 16.4g
CARBOHYDRATE 39g
FIBER 1.8g
CHOLESTEROL 34mg
IRON 3.3mg
SODIUM 732mg
CALCIUM 56mg

TIP: Measure any short, dry pasta, such as macaroni, penne, or orzo, in dry measuring cups.

2 cups uncooked penne (tube-shaped pasta)
Cooking spray
3 links hot Italian turkey sausage (about 12 ounces), cut into ½-inch slices
1 (16-ounce) package frozen bell pepper and onion stir-fry
1 (14.5-ounce) can diced tomatoes with basil, garlic, and oregano, undrained
½ teaspoon black pepper
Preshredded fresh Parmesan cheese (optional)

1. Cook pasta according to package directions, omitting salt and fat. Drain pasta, and set aside.

2. While pasta cooks, heat a large nonstick skillet over medium-high heat; coat pan with cooking spray. Add sausage, and cook 5 minutes or until browned, stirring often. Add bell pepper stir-fry, and cook 3 minutes or until bell pepper and onion are hot, stirring often. Add tomatoes and black pepper. Bring to a boil; reduce heat, and simmer 5 minutes.

3. Place pasta in a large bowl. Add sausage mixture, and toss. Divide among plates; top with cheese, if desired. Yield: 6 servings (serving size: about 1⅓ cups pasta).

prep: 9 minutes ∞ **cook:** 27 minutes

Stewed Lima Beans and Okra with Sausage

Using frozen vegetables cuts the prep time of this meal. There's no need to thaw the vegetables. They'll thaw quickly when they're added to the other hot ingredients.

- 1 teaspoon olive oil
- 8 ounces turkey kielbasa (such as Healthy Choice), cut into ¼-inch slices
- 2 garlic cloves, minced
- ¾ cup chopped onion
- ¼ cup chopped green bell pepper
- ½ cup chopped celery (about 1 stalk)
- 1 cup frozen whole-kernel corn
- 1¾ cups frozen baby lima beans
- 1 (14.5-ounce) can petite diced tomatoes, undrained
- ⅓ cup fat-free, less-sodium chicken broth
- 2 cups frozen cut okra
- ½ teaspoon chopped fresh thyme
- ½ teaspoon salt
- ¼ teaspoon freshly ground black pepper
- ¾ teaspoon hot sauce
- 2½ cups hot cooked rice
- ¼ cup chopped green onions (about 1)
- Additional hot sauce (optional)

1. Heat oil in a Dutch oven over medium-high heat. Add sausage; sauté 3 minutes. Add garlic and next 3 ingredients, and sauté 6 to 8 minutes or until tender. Stir in corn and next 8 ingredients; bring to a boil.

2. Cover, reduce heat, and simmer 12 to 15 minutes or until okra is tender, stirring occasionally. Uncover and cook 5 minutes. Divide rice among plates. Top with lima bean mixture, and sprinkle with green onions. Serve with additional hot sauce, if desired. Yield: 5 servings (serving size: ½ cup rice and 1 cup lima bean mixture).

***POINTS* value: 6**

per serving:
CALORIES 310
FAT 4g (saturated fat 1.1g)
PROTEIN 15g
CARBOHYDRATE 54.8g
FIBER 8.8g
CHOLESTEROL 20mg
IRON 4.1mg
SODIUM 799mg
CALCIUM 124mg

TIP: One cup of uncooked rice will yield about 3 cups of cooked rice. A rule of thumb is to use 2 cups of water per 1 cup of uncooked rice.

prep: 9 minutes ∞ **cook:** 34 minutes

Low-Country Boil

Plan to serve this all-in-one meal on your deck or patio along with plenty of napkins. Cover the tabletop with newspaper or brown paper to make cleanup a snap.

***POINTS* value: 6**

per serving:
CALORIES 315
FAT 5.8g (saturated fat 1.8g)
PROTEIN 31.5g
CARBOHYDRATE 31.9g
FIBER 2.7g
CHOLESTEROL 173mg
IRON 4.1mg
SODIUM 885mg
CALCIUM 60mg

TIP: Sprinkle Cajun seasoning over your serving if you want more spice. If you're watching your sodium intake, be aware that Cajun seasonings contain salt. Look for a salt-free version to use instead.

- 3 quarts water
- 2 lemons, cut in half
- 4 bay leaves
- 8 garlic cloves, sliced
- 1 (3-ounce) package crab boil
- 1 onion, cut into 8 wedges
- 2 (12-ounce) bottles light lager (such as Sam Adams)
- 1 teaspoon salt
- 10 small red potatoes, cut in half
- 2 (14-ounce) packages turkey kielbasa sausage (such as Healthy Choice), cut into 20 pieces
- 5 ears of corn, quartered
- 2 pounds unpeeled large shrimp

1. Combine first 8 ingredients in a large stockpot; bring to a boil. Add potatoes; reduce heat, and simmer 7 minutes. Add sausage, and cook 6 minutes. Add corn; cook 7 minutes. Add shrimp; cook 2 minutes.

2. Remove from heat. Drain; discard lemon halves, bay leaves, and crab boil. Serve immediately. Yield: 10 servings (serving size: 2 potato halves, 2 pieces sausage, 2 pieces corn, and about 4 shrimp).

prep: 8 minutes ∞ **cook:** 32 minutes

Salmon and Potato Bake

Tangy capers and fresh dill pair well with salmon and potatoes to make this a satisfying stand-alone recipe, but steamed fresh asparagus would make a nice accompaniment.

- 1 (20-ounce) package refrigerated sliced potatoes (such as Simply Potatoes)
- 2 tablespoons chopped fresh dill, divided
- 1 tablespoon plus 1 teaspoon olive oil, divided
- 1 garlic clove, minced
- ½ teaspoon salt, divided
- ½ teaspoon freshly ground black pepper, divided
- Cooking spray
- 4 (6-ounce) salmon fillets (1 to 1½ inches thick)
- 2 tablespoons capers, drained
- 4 lemon wedges

1. Preheat oven to 425°.

2. Combine potatoes, 1 tablespoon dill, 1 tablespoon olive oil, garlic, and ¼ teaspoon each of salt and pepper in a 13 x 9–inch baking dish coated with cooking spray, tossing to coat well. Spread potatoes in an even layer.

3. Bake at 425° for 20 to 22 minutes or until potatoes are browned on edges.

4. Rub fish evenly with remaining 1 teaspoon olive oil; sprinkle fish with remaining 1 tablespoon dill and remaining ¼ teaspoon each of salt and pepper. Place fish on top of potatoes; top with capers.

5. Bake at 425° for 12 to 14 minutes or until fish flakes easily when tested with a fork. Squeeze a lemon wedge over each serving. Yield: 4 servings (serving size: 1 salmon fillet, about ¾ cup potatoes, and 1 lemon wedge).

***POINTS* value: 7**

per serving:
CALORIES 338
FAT 10.6g (saturated fat 1.6g)
PROTEIN 37.1g
CARBOHYDRATE 23.2g
FIBER 1.6g
CHOLESTEROL 88mg
IRON 1.9mg
SODIUM 749mg
CALCIUM 30mg

TIP: If fresh seafood is on your shopping list, make the seafood department your last stop before heading for the checkout line.

prep: 7 minutes ∞ **cook:** 37 minutes ∞ **other:** 5 minutes

Skillet Lasagna

pictured on page 128

A traditional lasagna can take over 30 minutes of prep time and an hour to cook. For our version, we've streamlined the ingredients and cut the prep time to seven minutes.

***POINTS* value: 7**

per serving:
CALORIES 298
FAT 12.6g (saturated fat 6.4g)
PROTEIN 21g
CARBOHYDRATE 24.3g
FIBER 1.4g
CHOLESTEROL 62mg
IRON 2.6mg
SODIUM 857mg
CALCIUM 251mg

TIP: No-boil (or "oven ready") lasagna noodles are a great time-saver because there is no need to preboil them. The pasta absorbs liquid from the tomatoes during cooking to produce flavorful and tender noodles.

- ½ pound ground round
- ¼ cup chopped onion
- ½ teaspoon minced garlic
- 2 tablespoons balsamic vinegar
- 2 teaspoons Italian seasoning, divided
- 1 cup part-skim ricotta cheese
- 4 dried precooked lasagna noodles, broken into large pieces
- 1 (14.5-ounce) can diced tomatoes with basil, garlic, and oregano, undrained
- 1 cup bottled roasted red bell peppers, chopped
- 5 teaspoons commercial pesto
- ½ cup (2 ounces) preshredded mozzarella-Parmesan cheese blend

1. Cook first 3 ingredients in a large nonstick skillet over medium-high heat until beef is browned, stirring to crumble beef. Add vinegar and 1 teaspoon Italian seasoning. Spoon ricotta cheese evenly over beef. Top with lasagna noodles, making 1 flat layer (noodles will overlap).

2. Combine tomatoes and bell peppers, and spread over noodles, making sure that noodles are completely covered. Sprinkle with remaining 1 teaspoon Italian seasoning. Dollop pesto evenly over top. Bring mixture to a boil. Cover, reduce heat to low, and simmer 30 minutes or until noodles are soft. Uncover and sprinkle with cheese; let stand 5 minutes. Cut into wedges. Remove from pan with a slotted spatula. Yield: 5 servings (serving size: 1 wedge).

prep: 2 minutes ∞ **cook:** 50 minutes

Shepherd's Pie

You don't need to thaw the vegetables before adding them to the meat mixture. If you prefer mashed potatoes with the skins on, use homestyle refrigerated mashed potatoes. You can also substitute 3 cups of Buttermilk-Chive Mashed Potatoes (page 162).

- 1 teaspoon olive oil
- 1 small onion, diced
- 1½ pounds ground round
- 2 cups frozen mixed vegetables
- 3 tablespoons tomato paste
- ½ teaspoon salt
- ¼ teaspoon black pepper
- 1 (14-ounce) can fat-free, less-sodium beef broth
- 2 tablespoons all-purpose flour
- 1 (20-ounce) package refrigerated mashed potatoes (such as Simply Potatoes)

1. Preheat oven to 375°.

2. Heat oil in a large skillet over medium-high heat. Add onion; sauté 5 minutes. Add beef, and cook until beef is browned, stirring to crumble. Drain.

3. Return beef mixture to pan. Add mixed vegetables and next 3 ingredients; cook over medium heat 5 minutes or until vegetables are hot, stirring frequently. Combine broth and flour, stirring with a whisk.

4. Add broth mixture to beef mixture. Bring to a boil, and cook 3 minutes or until thick, stirring constantly.

5. Spoon beef mixture into an 11 x 8–inch baking dish. Spread potatoes over meat mixture, and fluff with a fork. Bake at 375° for 20 minutes or until browned. Yield: 6 servings (serving size: 1⅓ cups).

***POINTS* value: 5**

per serving:
CALORIES 285
FAT 6.2g (saturated fat 1.7g)
PROTEIN 29.4g
CARBOHYDRATE 31g
FIBER 5g
CHOLESTEROL 60mg
IRON 3mg
SODIUM 742mg
CALCIUM 38mg

TIP: If you don't have an 11 x 8–inch baking dish, use a 2-quart casserole. The baking time will be the same.

prep: 6 minutes ∞ **cook:** 39 minutes

Tamale Pie

pictured on page 115

Serve this hearty dish with some vegetables that have a *POINTS* value of 0, such as steamed zucchini and sliced summer-ripe tomatoes.

***POINTS* value: 6**

per serving:
CALORIES 326
FAT 7.1g (saturated fat 3.2g)
PROTEIN 23.5g
CARBOHYDRATE 42.6g
FIBER 3.6g
CHOLESTEROL 83mg
IRON 4.4mg
SODIUM 800mg
CALCIUM 149mg

TIP: On the weekend or whenever you have more time, chop all the onions you'll need for the week. Store the chopped onion in airtight containers in the refrigerator.

1 pound ground round
½ cup chopped onion
1 garlic clove, minced
1 (15-ounce) can pinto beans, rinsed and drained
1½ cups water
1 cup salsa
1½ tablespoons salt-free Mexican seasoning
1 cup all-purpose flour
¾ cup yellow cornmeal
1 tablespoon sugar
2 teaspoons baking powder
½ teaspoon salt
⅔ cup fat-free milk
1½ tablespoons butter, melted
1 large egg, beaten
Reduced-fat sour cream (optional)

1. Preheat oven to 400°.

2. Cook first 3 ingredients in a large skillet over medium-high heat until beef is browned, stirring to crumble beef. Drain well; return to pan. Add pinto beans and next 3 ingredients. Bring to a boil; reduce heat, and simmer, uncovered, 5 minutes or until mixture thickens, stirring occasionally.

3. Lightly spoon flour into a dry measuring cup; level with a knife. Stir together flour and next 4 ingredients in a medium bowl. Add milk, butter, and egg; stir until well blended.

4. Spoon beef mixture into an 11 x 7–inch baking dish. Spoon batter over beef mixture, spreading evenly.

5. Bake at 400° for 24 minutes or until golden. Cut into 6 equal portions. Dollop sour cream on each serving, if desired. Yield: 6 servings (serving size: 1 [3½-inch] square).

prep: 6 minutes ∞ **cook:** 15 minutes

Beefy Chili

pictured on page 35

Use any leftover chili as the basis for dinner later in the week. Try spooning ½ cup of chili over a 6-ounce baked potato for a meal with a *POINTS* value of 5.

- 1 pound ground round
- 1¼ cups chopped onion (about 1 medium)
- 1 cup chopped green bell pepper (about 1 medium)
- 1 garlic clove, minced
- 1 (16-ounce) can dark red kidney beans, rinsed and drained
- 1 (14.5-ounce) can diced tomatoes, undrained
- 1¼ cups water
- 2 tablespoons chili powder
- 1 tablespoon tomato paste
- 1 teaspoon ground cumin
- ½ teaspoon salt
- ¼ teaspoon crushed red pepper

1. Cook first 4 ingredients in a large nonstick skillet over medium-high heat until beef is browned, stirring to crumble beef.

2. Add kidney beans and remaining ingredients. Bring to a boil, reduce heat, and simmer, uncovered, 7 minutes. Yield: 4 servings (serving size: 1½ cups).

***POINTS* value: 4**

per serving:
CALORIES 244
FAT 4.6g (saturated fat 1.6g)
PROTEIN 29.4g
CARBOHYDRATE 23.1g
FIBER 7.5g
CHOLESTEROL 60mg
IRON 3.4mg
SODIUM 780mg
CALCIUM 52mg

TIP: Tomato paste is a richly flavored tomato concentrate that's perfect for adding hearty flavor to soups, stews, and pasta sauces. When a recipe calls for a small amount of paste, it's convenient to use paste from a tube, which can usually be found near the pasta sauces at your supermarket.

prep: 10 minutes ∞ **cook:** 15 minutes

Asian Pepper Steak

pictured on page 38

The thinner the slices of steak, the more tender and flavorful the meat will be. Freeze the steak for about 10 minutes so it can get firm before you slice it.

***POINTS* value: 6**

per serving:
CALORIES 275
FAT 6.8g (saturated fat 2.4g)
PROTEIN 20.3g
CARBOHYDRATE 32.5g
FIBER 1.1g
CHOLESTEROL 26mg
IRON 2.5mg
SODIUM 630mg
CALCIUM 27mg

TIP: Store fresh ginger wrapped tightly in plastic wrap in your refrigerator's vegetable crisper for up to three weeks.

2 (3½-ounce) bags uncooked boil-in-bag jasmine rice
1 pound flank steak, trimmed and cut diagonally against grain into wafer-thin slices
2 tablespoons all-purpose flour
1 teaspoon olive oil
2 tablespoons minced garlic
1 tablespoon minced fresh ginger
¼ teaspoon black pepper
1 medium green bell pepper, seeded and cut into strips (about 1¼ cups)
½ cup sliced onion
1 (14.5-ounce) can diced tomatoes, drained
¾ cup beef consommé
2 tablespoons soy sauce

1. Cook rice according to package directions, omitting salt and fat.

2. While rice cooks, combine flank steak and flour in a large zip-top plastic bag; seal bag, and toss to coat.

3. Heat oil in a large nonstick skillet over medium-high heat until hot. Add garlic and ginger; cook 1 minute, stirring constantly. Add steak and black pepper; cook 4 minutes, stirring occasionally to brown steak on all sides.

4. Add bell pepper strips and remaining ingredients. Cover; cook 4 minutes. Uncover; cook 3 minutes or until slightly thick, stirring occasionally. Serve over rice. Yield: 6 servings (serving size: ¾ cup steak mixture and ½ cup rice).

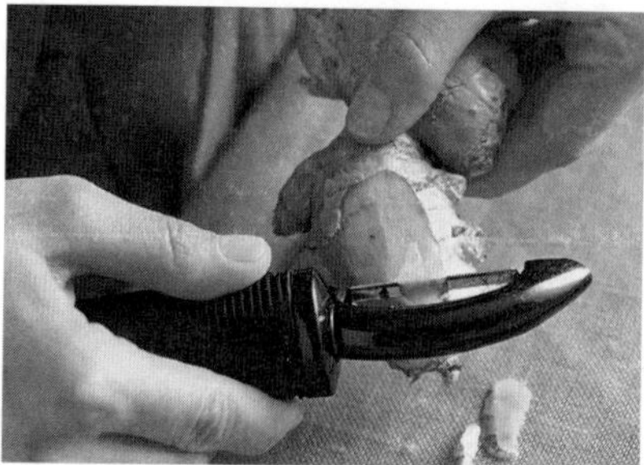

1. To peel fresh ginger, use a vegetable peeler or a paring knife to remove the tough skin and reveal the yellowish flesh.

2. Cut the peeled ginger into slices; then stack the slices, and cut into strips. Line up the strips, and cut crosswise into small pieces to mince.

prep: 2 minutes ∞ **cook:** 13 minutes

Mongolian Beef

This Asian meal with a *POINTS* value of 8 is hard to beat—it takes only 15 minutes from start to finish and uses a few simple ingredients that provide bold flavor.

- ½ cup uncooked instant brown rice
- 1 pound flank steak, trimmed and cut diagonally against grain into wafer-thin slices
- 1½ tablespoons cornstarch
- ⅓ cup low-sodium soy sauce
- ½ cup water
- ⅓ cup firmly packed light brown sugar
- 1 tablespoon canola oil
- 1 tablespoon minced garlic
- ½ teaspoon minced fresh ginger
- 3 green onions, cut into 2-inch pieces

1. Prepare rice according to package directions, omitting salt and fat.

2. While rice cooks, combine steak and cornstarch; set aside.

3. Combine soy sauce, water, and brown sugar in a small bowl; set aside.

4. Heat oil in a large nonstick skillet over medium-high heat. Add garlic and ginger, and sauté 1 minute. Add steak, and cook 4 minutes, stirring occasionally to brown on all sides. Add soy sauce mixture to pan, and cook 5 minutes or until sauce begins to thicken. Add onions; cook 1 minute. Serve with brown rice. Yield: 4 servings (serving size: ¾ cup beef mixture and ½ cup rice).

***POINTS* value: 8**

per serving:
CALORIES 354
FAT 12.3g (saturated fat 3.6g)
PROTEIN 26.6g
CARBOHYDRATE 32g
FIBER 0.8g
CHOLESTEROL 40mg
IRON 2.5mg
SODIUM 878mg
CALCIUM 57mg

TIP: Bottled minced garlic and minced ginger are available in your grocery's produce section. Their flavors aren't as robust as freshly minced garlic or ginger, but these products can save on prep time.

prep: 12 minutes ∞ **cook:** 1 hour and 10 minutes ∞ **other:** 5 minutes

Braised Steak with Mushrooms and Sour Cream

pictured on page 40

You'll have time to read the paper or help with homework while dinner simmers on the stove.

***POINTS* value: 9**

per serving:

CALORIES 393
FAT 14.8g (saturated fat 5.3g)
PROTEIN 28.5g
CARBOHYDRATE 34.8g
FIBER 2g
CHOLESTEROL 89mg
IRON 4.8mg
SODIUM 679mg
CALCIUM 65mg

TIP: Egg noodles take only about five minutes to cook once the water comes to a boil. Add the noodles to the boiling water as soon as you remove the steak mixture from the heat so that everything will be ready to serve at the same time.

3 tablespoons all-purpose flour, divided
⅛ teaspoon salt
⅛ teaspoon freshly ground black pepper
1 pound lean boneless sirloin steak, cut into 1-inch cubes
2 teaspoons olive oil
1 cup chopped onion
3 garlic cloves, minced
2 (8-ounce) packages presliced mushrooms
1 (14-ounce) can fat-free, less-sodium beef broth, divided
1 tablespoon stone-ground mustard
½ teaspoon dried thyme
½ teaspoon salt
¼ teaspoon freshly ground black pepper
⅓ cup reduced-fat sour cream
2 cups cooked egg noodles (about 1⅔ cups uncooked)

1. Combine 2 tablespoons flour, ⅛ teaspoon salt, and ⅛ teaspoon pepper in a zip-top plastic bag; add steak. Seal and shake well to coat.

2. Heat oil in a large Dutch oven over medium-high heat; add steak, browning on all sides. Add onion, garlic, and mushrooms; sauté 5 minutes.

3. Combine 2 tablespoons broth and remaining 1 tablespoon flour; stir well with a whisk.

4. Add remaining broth, mustard, and next 3 ingredients to steak mixture in pan. Bring to a boil; cover, reduce heat, and simmer 45 minutes.

5. Stir in broth mixture; simmer, uncovered, 10 minutes. Remove from heat, and let stand 5 minutes. Stir in sour cream. Serve over noodles. Yield: 4 servings (serving size: about 1¼ cups steak mixture and ½ cup cooked noodles).

prep: 2 minutes ∞ cook: 32 minutes

Red Beans and Rice

Our version of this classic Cajun dish replaces the higher-fat sausage with lean ham. Leftovers are even better the next day.

- 2 teaspoons olive oil
- Cooking spray
- 2 cups cubed ham
- 1½ cups frozen chopped onion, thawed
- 1 teaspoon bottled minced garlic
- 1½ cups uncooked converted rice
- 1 bay leaf
- ½ teaspoon dried thyme
- ½ teaspoon dried oregano
- ½ teaspoon ground red pepper
- 2 (14-ounce) cans fat-free, less-sodium chicken broth
- 2 (15.5-ounce) cans red kidney beans, rinsed and drained
- 1 (14.5-ounce) can diced tomatoes, undrained

1. Heat oil in a Dutch oven coated with cooking spray over medium-high heat. Add ham, and sauté 3 minutes. Stir in onion and garlic; sauté 4 minutes or until tender. Add rice and next 4 ingredients; sauté 30 seconds. Stir in remaining ingredients.

2. Bring to a boil; cover, reduce heat, and simmer 20 minutes or until liquid is absorbed and rice is tender. Discard bay leaf before serving. Yield: 7 servings (serving size: about 1½ cups).

***POINTS* value: 5**

per serving:
CALORIES 292
FAT 3.6g (saturated fat 0.8g)
PROTEIN 16.6g
CARBOHYDRATE 48.5g
FIBER 5.1g
CHOLESTEROL 19mg
IRON 3.1mg
SODIUM 870mg
CALCIUM 51mg

TIP: Cooking rice with other ingredients in a large pot can be tricky. For the best results, use converted (parboiled) rice. Instead of sticking together, the grains will stay separate when cooked. Don't confuse it with instant rice—converted rice takes longer to cook.

prep: 5 minutes ∞ **cook:** 21 minutes

Spinach and Potato Frittata

Eggs don't have to be served only at breakfast. A simple supper of eggs, cheese, and potatoes can be very satisfying. Round out your meal with 1½ cups of fresh strawberries for an additional *POINTS* value of 1.

***POINTS* value: 7**

per serving:
CALORIES 306
FAT 14.6g (saturated fat 4.7g)
PROTEIN 21.8g
CARBOHYDRATE 25.1g
FIBER 2g
CHOLESTEROL 121mg
IRON 1.9mg
SODIUM 422mg
CALCIUM 359mg

2 tablespoons olive oil
1 (20-ounce) package refrigerated hash brown potatoes (such as Simply Potatoes)
1 cup finely chopped onion
½ (6-ounce) package fresh baby spinach, chopped
1 teaspoon minced garlic
½ teaspoon salt
½ teaspoon freshly ground black pepper
1 cup egg substitute
3 large eggs
2 tablespoons 1% low-fat milk
3 (2.2-ounce) slices reduced-fat Swiss cheese, sliced in half diagonally

1. Preheat broiler.

2. Heat oil in a large ovenproof skillet. Add potatoes and onion; cook 10 minutes or until potatoes begin to brown, stirring occasionally. Add spinach and next 3 ingredients; cook 2 minutes.

3. Combine egg substitute, eggs, and milk, stirring with a whisk; pour over potato mixture. Cook 2 minutes. Arrange cheese on top in a spoke fashion.

4. Broil 6 minutes or until egg is set and cheese melts. Cut into 6 wedges. Yield: 6 servings (serving size: 1 wedge).

TIP: Use a cast-iron or heavy stainless-steel skillet for this recipe. Many nonstick skillets have plastic handles that can't withstand temperatures higher than 375°, even if you wrap the handle with foil.

prep: 15 minutes ∞ **cook:** 46 minutes ∞ **other:** 15 minutes

Spinach and Feta Quiche

Spinach and reduced-fat feta cheese pair well with eggs to create this delicious and savory quiche. Serve with a mixed green salad or fresh orange slices, if desired.

- ½ (15-ounce) package refrigerated pie dough (such as Pillsbury)
- 1 teaspoon olive oil
- 1 cup finely chopped onion
- 2 teaspoons bottled minced garlic
- 1 (10-ounce) package frozen chopped spinach, thawed, drained, and squeezed dry
- 1 (6-ounce) package reduced-fat feta cheese, crumbled
- 2 large eggs
- 1 cup 1% low-fat milk
- ½ teaspoon salt
- ½ teaspoon freshly ground black pepper

1. Preheat oven to 400°.

2. Unroll dough and fit into a 9-inch pie plate. Fold edges under, and flute. Bake at 400° on lowest oven rack for 8 minutes. Cool crust 15 minutes.

3. While crust cools, heat oil in a nonstick skillet over medium-high heat; add onion, and sauté 3 minutes. Add garlic; sauté 1 minute. Remove from heat; stir in spinach and feta. Combine eggs and next 3 ingredients, stirring with a whisk. Add to spinach mixture, stirring well. Pour filling into crust.

4. Bake at 400° on lowest oven rack for 33 minutes or until set. Shield edges of pie crust with foil during last 5 minutes of baking, if necessary. Cut into 6 wedges. Yield: 6 servings (serving size: 1 wedge).

***POINTS* value: 7**

per serving:
CALORIES 296
FAT 16.5g (saturated fat 7.4g)
PROTEIN 12.7g
CARBOHYDRATE 25.3g
FIBER 2.4g
CHOLESTEROL 88mg
IRON 1.4mg
SODIUM 796mg
CALCIUM 217mg

TIP: Baking on the bottom oven rack ensures a crisp crust in this meatless entrée.

prep: 4 minutes ∞ **cook:** 10 minutes

Black Bean Soup

There's no need to simmer this quick and easy soup for very long. It's full of fiber and flavor and is ready to serve after cooking only 10 minutes.

***POINTS* value: 4**

per serving:
CALORIES 207
FAT 2.9g (saturated fat 0.8g)
PROTEIN 11.8g
CARBOHYDRATE 28.4g
FIBER 8.9g
CHOLESTEROL 3mg
IRON 3.4mg
SODIUM 729mg
CALCIUM 98mg

TIP: Replace the reduced-fat cheese and reduced-fat sour cream with fat-free versions to make this a Core Plan ☑ recipe.

Cooking spray
½ cup frozen chopped onion
1 teaspoon bottled minced garlic
2 (15-ounce) cans black beans, rinsed and drained
1 (8¾-ounce) can whole-kernel corn, drained
½ cup refrigerated fresh salsa
1 (14-ounce) can fat-free, less-sodium beef broth
½ teaspoon ground cumin
¼ teaspoon ground red pepper
2 tablespoons fresh lime juice
¼ cup (1 ounce) preshredded reduced-fat 4-cheese Mexican blend cheese
Chopped fresh cilantro
Reduced-fat sour cream (optional)

1. Heat a large nonstick skillet over medium-high heat; coat pan with cooking spray. Add onion; cook 1 minute. Add garlic, and cook 3 minutes or until tender.

2. Mash 1 can of beans; add to onion and garlic. Add remaining can of beans, corn, and next 4 ingredients; bring to a boil. Reduce heat, and simmer, uncovered, until thoroughly heated. Stir in lime juice. Ladle soup into bowls; sprinkle with cheese and cilantro. Top with sour cream, if desired. Yield: 4 servings (serving size: 1¼ cups soup and 1 tablespoon cheese).

prep: 7 minutes ∞ **cook:** 15 minutes ∞ **other:** 15 minutes

Spicy Vegetarian Lasagna

Pantry staples such as salsa, black beans, and refried beans pack this lasagna with scrumptious Mexican flavors.

1 (16-ounce) bottle salsa
1½ teaspoons ground cumin
1 (8-ounce) can no-salt-added tomato sauce
Cooking spray
6 cooked lasagna noodles
1 (16-ounce) can fat-free refried beans
1 (15-ounce) can 50%-less-sodium black beans, rinsed and drained
1 cup (4 ounces) preshredded reduced-fat 4-cheese Mexican blend cheese
Reduced-fat sour cream (optional)

1. Preheat oven to 450°.

2. Combine first 3 ingredients; spread about ⅔ cup sauce in bottom of an 8-inch square baking dish coated with cooking spray. Arrange 2 noodles over sauce; spread half of refried beans over top. Sprinkle evenly with half of black beans. Top with ¼ cup cheese. Repeat layers once, placing last 2 noodles directly on cheese and topping with remaining ⅔ cup sauce. Sprinkle top with remaining ½ cup cheese.

3. Bake at 450° for 15 minutes or until sauce is bubbly. Let stand 15 minutes. Cut into 6 wedges. Top with sour cream, if desired. Yield: 6 servings (serving size: 1 [4 x 2½–inch] rectangle).

***POINTS* value: 5**

per serving:
CALORIES 267
FAT 3.7g (saturated fat 2.1g)
PROTEIN 17.1g
CARBOHYDRATE 44.4g
FIBER 9.2g
CHOLESTEROL 7mg
IRON 4mg
SODIUM 951mg
CALCIUM 220mg

TIP: Regular bottled salsa, which has a higher sodium content than fresh refrigerated salsa, is used in this recipe because the fresh version contains more liquid and would make this dish too runny.

prep: 20 minutes ∞ **cook:** 24 minutes

Peasant Garlic and Bean Soup with Sourdough Croutons

Look for peeled garlic cloves in the produce section of your grocery store to save on prep time for this hearty soup.

***POINTS* value: 4**

per serving:
CALORIES 226
FAT 1.2g (saturated fat 0.3g)
PROTEIN 13.1g
CARBOHYDRATE 42g
FIBER 6.6g
CHOLESTEROL 0mg
IRON 2.6mg
SODIUM 924mg
CALCIUM 111mg

TIP: Be careful when puréeing hot liquids in a blender. Hold a pot holder or towel over the lid when blending to keep it from popping off and splashing hot liquid on you.

- 2 cups cubed sourdough bread
- Olive oil–flavored cooking spray
- 1 tablespoon olive oil
- ¾ cup garlic cloves, slightly crushed (about 2 heads)
- 1½ cups chopped celery
- 1½ cups chopped onion
- 4 thyme sprigs
- 2 (16-ounce) cans navy beans, rinsed and drained
- 5½ cups fat-free, less-sodium chicken broth
- ½ teaspoon freshly ground black pepper
- Additional freshly ground black pepper
- Balsamic vinegar

1. Preheat oven to 425°.

2. Coat bread cubes with cooking spray. Bake at 425° for 8 to 10 minutes or until crisp; set aside.

3. While bread cubes bake, heat oil in a Dutch oven over medium-high heat. Add garlic and next 3 ingredients; cook 8 minutes or until vegetables are tender. Add beans and broth; bring to a boil. Cover, reduce heat, and simmer 10 minutes. Discard thyme sprigs, and add ½ teaspoon pepper. Place mixture in a blender or food processor; process until smooth.

4. Ladle into bowls. Top with croutons, additional pepper, and a drizzle of vinegar. Yield: 6 servings (serving size: 1½ cups).

prep: 6 minutes ∞ **cook:** 11 minutes

Polenta with Olives, Tomatoes, and Feta

pictured on page 39

Precooked refrigerated polenta is an excellent base for a quick vegetarian meal for two. You'll find it in the produce section of the supermarket in a variety of flavors.

Cooking spray
½ (16-ounce) package prepared refrigerated basil and garlic–flavored polenta (such as Marjon), cut into 6 slices
4 teaspoons chopped fresh oregano, divided
1 (14.5-ounce) can no-salt-added diced tomatoes, undrained
6 pitted kalamata olives, quartered
⅛ teaspoon freshly ground black pepper
½ cup crumbled reduced-fat feta cheese
Oregano sprigs (optional)

1. Heat a large nonstick skillet over medium-high heat; coat pan with cooking spray. Add polenta, and cook 4 to 5 minutes on each side or until browned. Remove from pan, and sprinkle polenta with 2 teaspoons chopped oregano; cover and keep warm.

2. Add tomatoes, olives, pepper, and remaining 2 teaspoons oregano to pan; bring to a boil. Reduce heat, and simmer 2 minutes or until thoroughly heated.

3. Place polenta slices in bowls; top with tomato mixture. Sprinkle evenly with feta cheese. Garnish with oregano sprigs, if desired. Yield: 2 servings (serving size: 3 polenta slices, ¾ cup tomato mixture, and ¼ cup feta cheese).

***POINTS* value: 4**

per serving:
CALORIES 216
FAT 7.1g (saturated fat 2.9g)
PROTEIN 10.2g
CARBOHYDRATE 26.2g
FIBER 4.5g
CHOLESTEROL 10mg
IRON 2.5mg
SODIUM 976mg
CALCIUM 97mg

TIP: To keep herbs fresh for up to one week, trim about ¼ inch from the stems, and rinse the herbs with cold water. Loosely wrap the herbs in a damp paper towel; then seal them in a zip-top plastic bag filled with air, and refrigerate.

prep: 7 minutes ∞ **cook:** 10 minutes ∞ **other:** 3 minutes

Spinach and Chickpea Rice with Feta

To make this meal even heartier, add 2 cups of leftover chopped cooked chicken for a *POINTS* value of 6 per serving.

***POINTS* value: 4**

per serving:
CALORIES 208
FAT 6.8g (saturated fat 1.6g)
PROTEIN 7.6g
CARBOHYDRATE 30.3g
FIBER 4.9g
CHOLESTEROL 5mg
IRON 2.2mg
SODIUM 555mg
CALCIUM 87mg

TIP: Chickpeas (also known as garbanzo beans) are an excellent source of magnesium and folate. They're also a good source of fiber and protein, which makes them quite filling.

- 1¾ cups water
- 1½ cups uncooked instant brown rice
- 2 teaspoons olive oil
- ¼ teaspoon salt
- ¾ cup (3 ounces) crumbled reduced-fat feta cheese
- 1 (6-ounce) package fresh baby spinach, coarsely chopped
- 1 (15-ounce) can chickpeas (garbanzo beans), rinsed and drained
- ¾ cup roasted red bell peppers, coarsely chopped
- ⅓ cup black olives, coarsely chopped
- 2 tablespoons lemon juice
- 1 teaspoon minced garlic
- ¼ teaspoon freshly ground black pepper

1. Place water in a large saucepan over medium-high heat, and bring to a boil. Stir in rice, oil, and salt; cover, reduce heat, and simmer 4 to 5 minutes or until water is absorbed and rice is tender.

2. Uncover and stir in feta cheese and remaining ingredients. Cover and let stand 3 minutes or until spinach wilts. Yield: 6 servings (serving size: about 1⅓ cups).

Speedy Sides

prep: 8 minutes ∞ **cook:** 2 minutes

Baby Arugula, Pear, and Gorgonzola Salad

pictured on page 124

Arugula is a peppery salad green that adds an extra "bite" to this salad. Baby spinach leaves would also work as a nice substitute, if desired. Serve this side along with Swordfish with Lemon-Thyme Butter (page 96) for a meal with a *POINTS* value of 7.

***POINTS* value: 2**

per serving:
CALORIES 88
FAT 3.2g (saturated fat 1.2g)
PROTEIN 2.2g
CARBOHYDRATE 14.7g
FIBER 2.5g
CHOLESTEROL 4mg
IRON 0.5mg
SODIUM 184mg
CALCIUM 71mg

TIP: Toasting the nuts helps bring a richer nutty taste to this delicious salad. For quick toasting, place the nuts in a dry skillet and cook them over medium heat, stirring frequently, for 1 to 2 minutes or until they are fragrant and golden.

2 Bartlett pears, cored and sliced
1 (5-ounce) package baby arugula
½ cup refrigerated fat-free raspberry vinaigrette (such as Naturally Fresh)
¼ cup (1 ounce) crumbled Gorgonzola cheese
2 tablespoons chopped walnuts, toasted
½ teaspoon freshly ground black pepper

1. Combine all ingredients in a large bowl; toss gently to coat. Serve immediately. Yield: 6 servings (serving size: 2 cups).

prep: 6 minutes

Broccoli Salad

Using light mayonnaise and fat-free yogurt lowers the fat and calories in this classic side salad. Reduced amounts of real bacon and cheese provide maximum flavor. If you prefer a bite of sweetness, mix in ¼ cup of golden raisins; the *POINTS* value per serving will not change.

- ⅓ cup light mayonnaise
- ¼ cup plain fat-free yogurt
- 3 tablespoons sugar
- 1 tablespoon white vinegar
- 1 (12-ounce) package broccoli florets, cut into bite-sized pieces
- 3 bacon slices, cooked and crumbled
- ⅓ cup chopped red onion
- ⅓ cup (1.3 ounces) shredded mild Cheddar cheese
- ¼ teaspoon freshly ground black pepper

1. Combine first 4 ingredients in a medium bowl. Add broccoli and remaining ingredients; toss gently to coat. Yield: 8 servings (serving size: ¾ cup).

***POINTS* value: 2**

per serving:
CALORIES 95
FAT 5.5g (saturated fat 1.9g)
PROTEIN 3.3g
CARBOHYDRATE 9.1g
FIBER 1.3g
CHOLESTEROL 10mg
IRON 0.4mg
SODIUM 152mg
CALCIUM 65mg

TIP: Spread the broccoli florets in a single layer on a cutting board and use a chef's knife to quickly chop the broccoli into smaller pieces.

prep: 6 minutes

Cucumber and Honeydew Salad ☑

pictured on page 36

Fresh mint, lime juice, and sweet honeydew melon make the perfect combination in this simple and refreshing side. The large serving size means this dish is especially satisfying.

***POINTS* value: 1**

per serving:
CALORIES 42
FAT 0.2g (saturated fat 0g)
PROTEIN 0.9g
CARBOHYDRATE 10.6g
FIBER 1.1g
CHOLESTEROL 0mg
IRON 0.4mg
SODIUM 89mg
CALCIUM 18mg

TIP: English (or seedless) cucumbers are usually twice the size of regular cucumbers. They also contain fewer seeds and have thinner skins. Substitute regular small cucumbers in this recipe, if desired.

2 cups cubed honeydew melon
2 cups chopped English cucumber
2 tablespoons chopped fresh mint
2 tablespoons freshly squeezed lime juice
2 tablespoons finely chopped red onion
⅛ teaspoon salt
Mint sprigs (optional)

1. Combine all ingredients in a large bowl; toss gently to coat.

2. Cover and chill until ready to serve. Garnish with mint sprigs, if desired. Yield: 4 servings (serving size: 1 cup).

prep: 2 minutes ∞ **cook:** 9 minutes

Grilled Nectarines with Blue Cheese

Take the heat out of the kitchen by preparing a quick and delicious weeknight supper on your grill. Serve this side along with Grilled Pork Medallions (page 103) for a meal with a *POINTS* value of 6.

- ½ cup light raspberry-walnut vinaigrette (such as Ken's Steak House)
- 3 tablespoons honey
- 4 ripe nectarines, halved and pitted
- 3 tablespoons sweetened dried cranberries
- Cooking spray
- 3 tablespoons crumbled blue cheese

1. Prepare grill.

2. Combine vinaigrette and honey in a small microwave-safe bowl. Brush vinaigrette mixture evenly over nectarine halves. Add dried cranberries to remaining vinaigrette mixture in bowl. Cover cranberry mixture with plastic wrap, and microwave at HIGH 1 minute or until mixture begins to boil. Set aside.

3. Place nectarines, cut sides down, on grill rack coated with cooking spray. Grill 4 to 6 minutes on each side or until nectarines are tender.

4. Place nectarines on a serving platter. Spoon about 1 teaspoon cranberries and 1 teaspoon vinaigrette mixture into center of each half. Sprinkle crumbled blue cheese evenly over nectarines. Serve warm. Yield: 8 servings (serving size: 1 nectarine half).

***POINTS* value: 2**

per serving:
CALORIES 115
FAT 4.2g (saturated fat 1.1g)
PROTEIN 1.5g
CARBOHYDRATE 20g
FIBER 1.4g
CHOLESTEROL 2mg
IRON 0.3mg
SODIUM 107mg
CALCIUM 22mg

TIP: Because of their hard center seeds, nectarines are considered to be a type of stone fruit. They begin to ripen in late June to early July and have thin skins that do not require peeling.

prep: 4 minutes ∞ **cook:** 5 minutes

Asparagus with Balsamic Butter

pictured on page 116

The rich combination of sweet balsamic vinegar, shallots, and light butter tossed with fresh asparagus creates a quick, delicious side dish to serve alongside Pesto and Roasted Pepper Fish Kebabs (page 91) or Blueberry-Balsamic Pork Cutlets (page 102).

***POINTS* value: 0**

per serving:
CALORIES 35
FAT 1.6g (saturated fat 0.9g)
PROTEIN 2.1g
CARBOHYDRATE 4.8g
FIBER 1.9g
CHOLESTEROL 4mg
IRON 2mg
SODIUM 172mg
CALCIUM 24mg

TIP: If you plan to heat up the grill to prepare an entrée, then save time and effort by grilling this asparagus, too. Grill the asparagus for four minutes or until crisp-tender. Toss with balsamic butter after grilling.

1¼ pounds asparagus spears
Cooking spray
2 tablespoons finely chopped shallots
1 tablespoon light stick butter
1 teaspoon balsamic vinegar
¼ teaspoon salt
¼ teaspoon freshly ground black pepper

1. Snap off tough ends of asparagus. Bring 1 inch of water to a boil in a large skillet; add asparagus. Cook 4 to 5 minutes or until crisp-tender. Drain and place on a serving platter.

2. While asparagus cooks, heat a large nonstick skillet over medium heat; coat pan with cooking spray. Add shallots; sauté 1 to 2 minutes or until soft. Remove from heat; stir in butter and balsamic vinegar. Pour balsamic butter over asparagus, and sprinkle with salt and pepper. Toss well. Yield: 4 servings (serving size: ¼ of asparagus).

prep: 10 minutes ∞ **cook:** 10 minutes

Grilled Chipotle-Lime Corn ☑

The spicy and smoky flavors of the chipotle seasoning helped this recipe score our Test Kitchens' highest rating. Grill your entire dinner and serve with Spicy Grilled Flank Steak with Peppers and Onions (page 64) for a meal with a *POINTS* value of 7.

1 teaspoon salt-free Southwest chipotle seasoning (such as Mrs. Dash)
1 teaspoon grated fresh lime rind
¼ teaspoon salt
1½ tablespoons fresh lime juice
4 medium ears corn

1. Prepare grill.

2. Combine first 4 ingredients in a small bowl. Place corn on a large plate; brush with lime mixture, reserving drippings on plate.

3. Grill corn 10 minutes, turning once or until corn is slightly charred and done. Return corn to plate, and brush with reserved drippings. Yield: 4 servings (serving size: 1 ear of corn).

***POINTS* value: 2**

per serving:
CALORIES 79
FAT 1.7g (saturated fat 0.3g)
PROTEIN 3.9g
CARBOHYDRATE 17.7g
FIBER 2.5g
CHOLESTEROL 0mg
IRON 0.5mg
SODIUM 159mg
CALCIUM 3mg

TIP: Salt-free seasoning blends are a terrific way to add extra flavor and control the amount of sodium in a dish. Our recipe also calls for a small amount of salt, but since we didn't use a regular seasoning blend, the sodium level will still be low.

prep: 4 minutes ∞ **cook:** 15 minutes

Italian Green Beans ☑

Your family will never guess that this fresh-tasting, boldly flavored recipe uses canned green beans. Serve with Seared Chicken Breast with Pan Gravy (page 85) for a meal with a *POINTS* value of 8.

***POINTS* value: 2**

per serving:
CALORIES 118
FAT 2.8g (saturated fat 0.3g)
PROTEIN 2.1g
CARBOHYDRATE 20.4g
FIBER 4.1g
CHOLESTEROL 0mg
IRON 1.1mg
SODIUM 612mg
CALCIUM 45mg

TIP: Be careful when you sauté garlic; burnt garlic will add a bitter flavor to the finished dish.

- 2 teaspoons extravirgin olive oil
- 1 cup chopped onion
- 1 tablespoon bottled minced garlic
- 1 (14.5-ounce) can diced tomatoes with basil, garlic, and oregano, undrained
- 2 (14.5-ounce) cans cut Italian green beans, drained
- ½ teaspoon freshly ground black pepper

1. Heat oil in a large nonstick skillet over medium-high heat. Add onion; sauté 5 minutes or until tender. Add garlic; sauté 1 minute. Add tomatoes; bring to a boil. Reduce heat, and simmer, uncovered, 5 minutes. Add green beans and pepper; cook 2 minutes or until thoroughly heated. Yield: 4 servings (serving size: 1 cup).

prep: 10 minutes ∞ **cook:** 8 minutes ∞ **other:** 30 minutes

Grilled Okra ☑

pictured on page 44

Grilling adds a whole new taste sensation to veggies, especially when they take on a grilled flavor and look. Purchase firm and brightly colored okra pods that are less than four inches long; they may be more tender than the larger ones.

- 16 (12-inch) wooden skewers
- 1 pound small okra pods
- 1 tablespoon extravirgin olive oil
- 1 teaspoon minced garlic
- ½ teaspoon salt
- ½ teaspoon freshly ground black pepper

1. Soak skewers in water 30 minutes.

2. Prepare grill.

3. Divide okra evenly among skewers (thread okra with 2 skewers to ease grilling). Combine olive oil and next 3 ingredients; brush over okra.

4. Grill over medium-high heat 4 to 6 minutes on each side or until crisp-tender. Serve immediately. Yield: 4 servings (serving size: 2 skewers).

***POINTS* value: 1**

per serving:
CALORIES 67
FAT 3.6g (saturated fat 0.5g)
PROTEIN 2.4g
CARBOHYDRATE 8.4g
FIBER 3.7g
CHOLESTEROL 0mg
IRON 0.9mg
SODIUM 300mg
CALCIUM 94mg

TIP: Use long-handled tongs to easily turn the double-skewered okra pods. A grill basket can be used to grill the okra, too.

prep: 3 minutes ∞ **cook:** 8 minutes

Buttermilk-Chive Mashed Potatoes

Our version of this family-friendly side captures the flavor and creaminess of traditional recipes but saves time by using packaged frozen mashed potatoes. Serve this hearty side with Barbecue Meat Loaf (page 99) for a meal with a *POINTS* value of 7.

***POINTS* value: 3**

per serving:
CALORIES 131
FAT 4.8g (saturated fat 1.8g)
PROTEIN 4g
CARBOHYDRATE 17.6g
FIBER 1.6g
CHOLESTEROL 11mg
IRON 0.3mg
SODIUM 89mg
CALCIUM 73mg

TIP: Since this recipe makes a large yield, it is a perfect make-ahead recipe to use in our Shepherd's Pie (page 139).

1 (22-ounce) package frozen mashed potatoes
2⅓ cups low-fat buttermilk
½ cup reduced-fat sour cream
3 tablespoons yogurt-based spread (such as Brummel & Brown)
½ teaspoon freshly ground black pepper
¼ cup chopped fresh chives

1. Combine first 5 ingredients in a large microwave-safe serving bowl. Cover and microwave at HIGH 5 minutes; stir well. Microwave at HIGH an additional 3 to 5 minutes or until thoroughly heated. Stir in chives. Yield: 11 servings (serving size: about ½ cup).

prep: 2 minutes ∞ **cook:** 20 minutes

Curried Potatoes and Peas ☑

Refrigerated potato wedges will help you get a jump start when preparing weeknight meals. Look for these versatile and time-saving potatoes in the dairy case of your supermarket. Serve with broiled lamb chops or fish.

- 1 tablespoon extravirgin olive oil
- 1½ cups thinly sliced onion
- 1 (1-pound, 4-ounce) bag refrigerated red potato wedges (such as Simply Potatoes)
- 1 teaspoon minced garlic
- 1 (14.5-ounce) can diced tomatoes, undrained
- ½ cup fat-free, less-sodium chicken broth
- 1 tablespoon hot curry powder
- ½ teaspoon salt
- 1 cup frozen petite green peas
- ½ cup plain fat-free yogurt

1. Heat oil in a large nonstick skillet over medium-high heat. Add onion; sauté 2 minutes, stirring occasionally. Add potatoes; sauté 5 minutes, stirring occasionally. Add garlic; sauté 1 minute. Add diced tomatoes and next 3 ingredients; cover and cook 10 minutes or until potatoes are tender.

2. Stir in peas and yogurt; cook until thoroughly heated. Yield: 10 servings (serving size: ½ cup).

***POINTS* value: 1**

per serving:
CALORIES 82
FAT 1.6g (saturated fat 0.2g)
PROTEIN 3.4g
CARBOHYDRATE 14.3g
FIBER 3.1g
CHOLESTEROL 0.3mg
IRON 0.8mg
SODIUM 280mg
CALCIUM 32mg

TIP: There's no need to thaw the green peas before adding them to the skillet. They'll cook quickly when they're added to the hot potato mixture.

prep: 8 minutes ∞ **cook:** 20 minutes

Pesto-Vegetable Medley

pictured on page 48

Serve this easy side for dinner with grilled or roasted meat and as a cold potato salad for lunch the next day.

***POINTS* value: 2**

per serving:
CALORIES 100
FAT 3.2g (saturated fat 0.8g)
PROTEIN 3.3g
CARBOHYDRATE 15.5g
FIBER 2.7g
CHOLESTEROL 2mg
IRON 1.1mg
SODIUM 202mg
CALCIUM 67mg

TIP: Look for pretrimmed green beans in your grocery's produce section. Or purchase about 1 pound of green beans and then use a chef's knife to quickly trim the tops and tips from the beans.

2 pounds red potatoes, unpeeled and halved (or quartered if large)
1 (12-ounce) package pretrimmed green beans
Cooking spray
1 pint grape tomatoes
5 tablespoons commercial pesto
3⁄4 teaspoon salt
1⁄4 teaspoon freshly ground black pepper

1. Place potatoes in a Dutch oven or large saucepan, and cover with water. Bring to a boil; reduce heat, cover, and cook 6 minutes. Add green beans; cook 8 minutes or until potatoes are tender and beans are crisp-tender. Drain; place potatoes in a large serving bowl, and set aside.

2. Wipe pan with a paper towel. Spray pan with cooking spray, and place over medium heat. Add tomatoes, and sauté 1 to 2 minutes or until tomatoes begin to brown slightly. Add to potatoes and green beans.

3. Combine pesto, salt, and pepper. Spoon over vegetable mixture, and toss gently to coat. Serve warm or at room temperature. Yield: 12 servings (serving size: 1 cup).

prep: 8 minutes ⚭ cook: 20 minutes

Roasted Sweet Potatoes

Curry, cinnamon, and nutmeg complement the natural sweetness of the potatoes and cranberries. Serve with center-cut ham steaks or roasted turkey breast.

- 1/4 teaspoon salt
- 1/4 teaspoon freshly ground black pepper
- 1/4 teaspoon ground cinnamon
- 1/8 teaspoon ground curry powder
- Dash of grated whole nutmeg
- 5 cups cubed peeled sweet potato (about 1 pound)
- 2 teaspoons olive oil
- Cooking spray
- 1/3 cup sweetened dried cranberries
- 1 tablespoon thawed orange juice concentrate
- 1/8 teaspoon salt

1. Preheat oven to 450°.

2. Combine first 5 ingredients in a small bowl.

3. Toss potato with olive oil and spice mixture until coated. Arrange potato in a 15 x 10–inch jelly-roll pan coated with cooking spray.

4. Bake at 450° for 20 to 25 minutes or until potato is tender and browned, stirring twice.

5. Remove from oven, and transfer to a serving bowl. Toss with cranberries, orange juice concentrate, and 1/8 teaspoon salt. Serve immediately. Yield: 7 servings (serving size: 1/2 cup).

***POINTS* value: 2**

per serving:
CALORIES 117
FAT 1.4g (saturated fat 0.2g)
PROTEIN 1.6g
CARBOHYDRATE 25g
FIBER 3.2g
CHOLESTEROL 0mg
IRON 0.6mg
SODIUM 177mg
CALCIUM 31mg

TIP: Keep an extra container of orange juice concentrate in your freezer and stir small amounts of it into savory and sweet dishes. Your dishes will have fresh orange flavor without you having to squeeze an orange.

prep: 10 minutes ∞ **cook:** 13 minutes

Quick Sweet Potato Casserole

By using light butter and decreasing the amount of syrup and pecans, we produced a sweet potato casserole with less fat and calories than the traditional kind—without sacrificing the sweet, rich taste. If you don't have any maple syrup, substitute honey or brown sugar.

***POINTS* value: 4**

per serving:
CALORIES 236
FAT 5.1g (saturated fat 1.2g)
PROTEIN 2.8g
CARBOHYDRATE 44.9g
FIBER 5.2g
CHOLESTEROL 4mg
IRON 1.1mg
SODIUM 174mg
CALCIUM 34mg

TIP: To keep the maple syrup from sticking to the measuring spoon, spray the spoon first with cooking spray.

- 4 sweet potatoes (about 2 pounds)
- 1½ tablespoons light stick butter
- ¼ teaspoon salt
- ⅛ teaspoon nutmeg
- ⅛ teaspoon freshly ground black pepper
- Cooking spray
- ¼ cup chopped pecans
- 3 tablespoons maple syrup

1. Scrub sweet potatoes; pat dry, and pierce several times with a small knife. Microwave potatoes at HIGH 10 minutes or until tender; cool slightly.

2. Peel potatoes, and place in a medium bowl. Add butter and next 3 ingredients. Beat potato mixture with a mixer at medium speed until smooth; spoon into a 1-quart baking dish coated with cooking spray. Sprinkle with pecans, and drizzle with maple syrup.

3. Preheat broiler.

4. Broil 6 inches from heat 3 to 4 minutes or until nuts are golden. Serve immediately. Yield: 6 servings (serving size: ½ cup).

prep: 7 minutes ∞ **cook:** 15 minutes

Creamed Spinach

We used light butter, light cream cheese, and reduced-fat white Cheddar cheese to decrease the fat but not the flavor in this comforting side dish. Serve with Teriyaki Tri-Tip (page 100) for a meal with a *POINTS* value of 8.

Cooking spray
2 (12-ounce) bags fresh baby spinach
1 tablespoon light stick butter
1/3 cup finely chopped onion
2 teaspoons bottled minced garlic
1 tablespoon all-purpose flour
1/4 cup fat-free milk
1/2 cup tub-style light cream cheese, softened
1/2 cup (2 ounces) reduced-fat shredded white Cheddar cheese (such as Kraft Cracker Barrel)
1/4 teaspoon freshly ground black pepper
1/4 teaspoon hot sauce

1. Heat a large Dutch oven over medium-high heat; coat pan with cooking spray. Add spinach; sauté 5 minutes or until wilted. Drain spinach in a colander, pressing spinach with back of a spoon to remove as much moisture as possible.

2. Melt butter in pan; sauté onion and garlic over medium heat 3 minutes or until tender. Add flour, and cook 1 minute, stirring constantly. Add milk and cheeses; cook 2 minutes or until cheese melts, stirring constantly. Add spinach; cook 3 minutes or until spinach is thoroughly heated. Remove from heat; stir in pepper and hot sauce. Yield: 4 servings (serving size: about 1/2 cup).

***POINTS* value: 3**

per serving:
CALORIES 159
FAT 7g (saturated fat 4.4g)
PROTEIN 11.5g
CARBOHYDRATE 12g
FIBER 4.3g
CHOLESTEROL 24mg
IRON 5.6mg
SODIUM 388mg
CALCIUM 302mg

TIP: Using bags of tender baby spinach saves you time, since the greens are ready to use. The stems on regular spinach leaves tend to be larger and tougher and need to be removed before cooking.

prep: 5 minutes ∞ **cook:** 8 minutes

Lemon-Herb Roasted Tomatoes ☑

This simple side dish is delicious and so easy to prepare. Roasting the grape tomatoes intensifies their natural flavor. Enjoy these delicious tomatoes with Grilled Swordfish Steaks with Sun-Dried Tomato Butter (page 95) for a meal with a *POINTS* value of 7.

***POINTS* value: 1**

per serving:
CALORIES 49
FAT 2.7g (saturated fat 0.4g)
PROTEIN 1.4g
CARBOHYDRATE 6.4g
FIBER 2.1g
CHOLESTEROL 0mg
IRON 0.6mg
SODIUM 153mg
CALCIUM 20mg

TIP: To quickly rinse and drain the tomatoes, use the plastic container they come in as a colander. Open the lid and place the container under a faucet of cold running water. The water will drain through the holes in the bottom.

2 pints grape tomatoes
¾ teaspoon dried thyme
½ teaspoon freshly ground black pepper
½ teaspoon grated fresh lemon rind
¼ teaspoon salt
2 teaspoons olive oil
1 teaspoon fresh lemon juice

1. Preheat oven to 475°.

2. Rinse tomatoes, and pat dry with paper towels; place in a large bowl.

3. Gently stir in thyme and remaining ingredients. Place tomato mixture in a single layer on a large jelly-roll pan.

4. Bake at 475° for 5 minutes. Gently shake pan, and bake an additional 3 to 5 minutes or until tomato skins are blistered and beginning to pop.
Yield: 4 servings (serving size: ¾ cup).

prep: 5 minutes ∞ **cook:** 10 minutes

Tomato and White Bean Gratin

Because their flavor is reminiscent of summer-ripe tomatoes, jarred diced tomatoes lend this dish a fresh taste. Sprinkle the bean and tomato mixture with breadcrumbs and Parmesan cheese for a flavorful topping. Serve with roasted pork, chicken, or turkey.

1 (15.5-ounce) can cannellini beans, rinsed and drained
1 (14.5-ounce) jar petite diced tomatoes with basil, garlic, and oregano (such as Del Monte Garden Select), drained
1 teaspoon bottled minced garlic
¼ teaspoon freshly ground black pepper
⅛ teaspoon salt
Cooking spray
½ cup panko (Japanese breadcrumbs)
¼ cup grated Parmesan cheese

1. Preheat oven to 425°.

2. Combine first 5 ingredients in an 8-inch square baking dish coated with cooking spray. Combine breadcrumbs and cheese; sprinkle over bean mixture. Lightly coat crumb mixture with cooking spray. Bake at 425° for 10 minutes or until golden. Yield: 6 servings (serving size: ½ cup).

***POINTS* value: 1**

per serving:
CALORIES 76
FAT 1.4g (saturated fat 0.6g)
PROTEIN 3.9g
CARBOHYDRATE 11.5g
FIBER 2.1g
CHOLESTEROL 3mg
IRON 0.7mg
SODIUM 307mg
CALCIUM 57mg

TIP: You'll find jars of diced tomatoes alongside the canned tomatoes in your supermarket. Canned diced tomatoes can be substituted, but the flavor will be different and the sodium may be higher.

prep: 11 minutes ∞ **cook:** 5 minutes ∞ **other:** 5 minutes

Curried Couscous

Couscous, a type of pasta, is low in fat, simple to make, and delicious served hot or cold. It can also be served as a side dish, a salad, or an entrée. This recipe yields 6 cups, so serve some tonight with Curried Salmon Steaks with Wilted Spinach (page 93) for a meal with a *POINTS* value of 7.

***POINTS* value: 2**

per serving:
CALORIES 125
FAT 1.2g (saturated fat 0.2g)
PROTEIN 4.2g
CARBOHYDRATE 25.6g
FIBER 2.1g
CHOLESTEROL 0mg
IRON 0.9mg
SODIUM 144mg
CALCIUM 19mg

TIP: Look for couscous on the grocery shelves near the rice and pasta.

2 cups organic vegetable broth (such as Swanson Certified Organic)
½ cup golden raisins
1 teaspoon curry powder
½ teaspoon garlic salt
½ teaspoon olive oil
¼ teaspoon ground cumin
¼ teaspoon freshly ground black pepper
1 cup frozen petite green peas
1 (10-ounce) box plain couscous
¼ cup thinly sliced green onions
5 teaspoons sliced almonds, toasted

1. Combine first 7 ingredients in a medium saucepan; bring to a boil over medium-high heat. Stir in peas and couscous; cover. Remove from heat; let stand 5 minutes. Add green onions and almonds; fluff gently with a fork. Yield: 12 servings (serving size: ½ cup).

prep: 2 minutes ⚮ **cook:** 11 minutes

Herbed Cheese Grits

The light garlic-and-herbs spreadable cheese adds flavor and creaminess to plain grits for a quick and satisfying side to serve with seared sirloin steak.

- 2 cups fat-free, less-sodium chicken broth
- ½ cup uncooked quick-cooking grits
- ¼ cup light garlic-and-herbs spreadable cheese (such as Alouette Light)
- ¼ teaspoon freshly ground black pepper

1. Bring broth to a boil in a medium saucepan over medium-high heat.

2. Slowly stir in ½ cup grits; cover, reduce heat, and simmer 5 minutes or until grits are thickened, stirring occasionally.

3. Stir in cheese and pepper. Cook 1 to 2 minutes or until cheese melts, stirring occasionally. Serve immediately. Yield: 4 servings (serving size: ½ cup).

POINTS **value: 2**

per serving:
CALORIES 75
FAT 2.2g (saturated fat 1.5g)
PROTEIN 3.2g
CARBOHYDRATE 16.1g
FIBER 0.3g
CHOLESTEROL 10mg
IRON 0.8mg
SODIUM 285mg
CALCIUM 2mg

TIP: Serve the remaining spreadable cheese with your favorite raw veggies for a quick snack. One tablespoon has a ***POINTS*** value of 1.

prep: 5 minutes ∞ **cook:** 18 minutes

Lemon-Garlic Linguine

Lemon juice, garlic, and extravirgin olive oil lend a delicate fresh taste to this quick and easy pasta dish. Serve with baked fish or chicken.

***POINTS* value: 3**

per serving:
CALORIES 125
FAT 2.3g (saturated fat 0.4g)
PROTEIN 3.9g
CARBOHYDRATE 21.7g
FIBER 1g
CHOLESTEROL 0mg
IRON 0.9mg
SODIUM 147mg
CALCIUM 6mg

TIP: When a recipe calls for both grated lemon rind and lemon juice, grate the lemon before squeezing it for the juice. To get the most juice, roll the lemon firmly between your palm and the countertop before squeezing.

- 8 ounces uncooked linguine
- 1 tablespoon extravirgin olive oil, divided
- 3 garlic cloves, minced
- 1 teaspoon grated fresh lemon rind
- 1 tablespoon fresh lemon juice
- ½ teaspoon salt
- ¼ teaspoon freshly ground black pepper

1. Cook pasta according to package directions, omitting salt and fat; drain and place in a bowl.

2. Heat a small nonstick skillet over medium heat. Add 1 teaspoon oil, garlic, and lemon rind. Cook 1 to 2 minutes, stirring constantly.

3. Add garlic mixture, remaining 2 teaspoons oil, lemon juice, salt, and pepper to pasta; toss well. Serve immediately. Yield: 8 servings (serving size: ½ cup).

Everyday Desserts

prep: 2 minutes ∞ **cook:** 5 minutes

Apple Crepes with Caramel Topping

Keep the ingredients for this dessert on hand so that you can quickly answer the question "What's for dessert?"

***POINTS* value: 6**

per serving:
CALORIES 313
FAT 4g (saturated fat 1g)
PROTEIN 3.7g
CARBOHYDRATE 63.2g
FIBER 2.1g
CHOLESTEROL 8mg
IRON 0.1mg
SODIUM 139mg
CALCIUM 69mg

TIP: Stock up on packages of frozen apples; they're ideal for quick desserts and side dishes.

1 (12-ounce) package frozen apples (such as Stouffer's Harvest Apples)
2 teaspoons brown sugar
¼ teaspoon apple pie spice
3 ready-to-use crepes (such as Frieda's)
1 cup vanilla low-fat ice cream
3 tablespoons fat-free caramel topping

1. Prepare apples according to package directions.

2. Sprinkle brown sugar and apple pie spice over apples; stir well. Spoon ⅓ cup apple mixture onto center of each crepe. Roll up crepes. Place crepes on a microwave-safe plate.

3. Microwave at HIGH 10 seconds or until heated.

4. Top each crepe with ⅓ cup ice cream and 1 tablespoon caramel topping. Serve immediately. Yield: 3 servings (serving size: 1 crepe).

prep: 15 minutes ∞ **cook:** 38 minutes

Individual Apple-Blueberry Crumbles

pictured on page 126

This recipe revamps the traditional fruit crisp by combining tart Granny Smith apples with sweet blueberries and baking each serving in an individual dish.

- ⅓ cup all-purpose flour
- ½ cup quick-cooking oats
- ⅓ cup packed light brown sugar
- ¼ teaspoon ground cinnamon
- ⅛ teaspoon salt
- ¼ cup chilled butter, cut into small pieces
- 4 cups chopped peeled Granny Smith apple (about 2 large apples)
- 1 pint fresh or frozen blueberries
- 2 tablespoons all-purpose flour
- 2 tablespoons light brown sugar
- 1 tablespoon fresh lemon juice
- Cooking spray

1. Preheat oven to 375°.

2. Lightly spoon ⅓ cup flour into a dry measuring cup; level with a knife. Combine ⅓ cup flour and next 4 ingredients. Using fingertips, rub chilled butter into flour mixture until crumbly.

3. Combine apple and next 4 ingredients. Place about ⅔ cup apple mixture in each of 6 (10-ounce) custard cups or ramekins coated with cooking spray, and sprinkle with oat mixture. Arrange custard cups on a 15 x 10–inch jelly-roll pan.

4. Bake at 375° for 38 minutes or until lightly browned and bubbly. Yield: 6 servings (serving size: 1 crumble).

***POINTS* value: 5**

per serving:
CALORIES 256
FAT 8.4g (saturated fat 4.9g)
PROTEIN 2.6g
CARBOHYDRATE 45.5g
FIBER 4.1g
CHOLESTEROL 20mg
IRON 1.3mg
SODIUM 110mg
CALCIUM 29mg

TIP: Buy blueberries when they're in season and are less expensive. Then freeze them to enjoy months later. Freeze the berries in a single layer on a baking sheet; then transfer them to a heavy-duty zip-top plastic bag.

prep: 15 minutes ∞ other: 2 hours

Banana Pudding

We reduced the fat and calories in traditional banana pudding by 50%, but our version is so creamy and luscious that no one will ever know it's light.

***POINTS* value: 5**

per serving:
CALORIES 254
FAT 6.3g (saturated fat 4.3g)
PROTEIN 5.4g
CARBOHYDRATE 44.6g
FIBER 1g
CHOLESTEROL 9mg
IRON 0.5mg
SODIUM 233mg
CALCIUM 129mg

TIP: Whisks are efficient tools for dissolving solids in liquids, beating egg whites, or blending salad dressings.

2 cups fat-free milk
1 (1-ounce) package sugar-free, fat-free vanilla instant pudding mix
1 (14-ounce) can fat-free sweetened condensed milk
½ cup (4 ounces) block-style ⅓-less-fat cream cheese, softened
1 (16-ounce) container frozen reduced-calorie whipped topping, thawed and divided
56 reduced-fat vanilla wafers
4 cups sliced ripe banana (about 4 bananas)

1. Combine fat-free milk and pudding mix in a medium bowl; stir with a whisk 2 minutes. In another bowl, combine sweetened condensed milk and cream cheese, stirring with a whisk until smooth. Fold in 1 cup whipped topping. Fold cream cheese mixture into pudding mixture until blended.

2. Arrange half of vanilla wafers in bottom of a 13 x 9–inch baking dish. Arrange half of banana slices over wafers. Spread half of pudding mixture over banana. Repeat procedure with remaining wafers, banana, and pudding mixture. Top with remaining whipped topping.

3. Cover and refrigerate 2 hours or until thoroughly chilled. Yield: 16 servings (serving size: about ¾ cup).

prep: 1 minute ∞ **cook:** 7½ minutes ∞ **other:** 5 minutes

Quick Summer Pudding

This classic summer dessert can be made at any time of the year, thanks to frozen berries.

- 1 (12-ounce) package frozen mixed berries
- ¼ cup sugar
- ¼ cup orange juice
- 4 (1-ounce) slices French bread, toasted
- ½ cup canned refrigerated fat-free dairy whipped topping (such as Reddi-wip)

1. Combine first 3 ingredients in a microwave-safe bowl, and microwave at HIGH 2½ minutes or until berries are thawed. Stir well.

2. Arrange toasted bread on a rimmed serving platter or in a baking dish with sides; pour berry mixture over bread. Let stand 5 minutes to allow berry juice to soak into bread. Serve with whipped topping. Yield: 4 servings (serving size: 1 slice bread, about ½ cup berry mixture, and 2 tablespoons whipped topping).

***POINTS* value: 4**

per serving:
CALORIES 209
FAT 1.2g (saturated fat 0.2g)
PROTEIN 4g
CARBOHYDRATE 45g
FIBER 3.6g
CHOLESTEROL 0mg
IRON 1.4mg
SODIUM 225mg
CALCIUM 41mg

TIP: Any type of crusty sourdough bread can be substituted for the French bread. Just be sure to cut the bread into 1-ounce slices.

prep: 10 minutes ∞ **other:** 30 minutes

Key Lime–Strawberry Tarts

These delicious no-cook desserts are sweet, tart, and creamy—the perfect combination when you crave a fuss-free treat.

***POINTS* value: 5**

per serving:
CALORIES 227
FAT 6.1g (saturated fat 1g)
PROTEIN 3.7g
CARBOHYDRATE 38.4g
FIBER 1.5g
CHOLESTEROL 4mg
IRON 0.5mg
SODIUM 184mg
CALCIUM 89mg

TIP: You can find bottled Key lime juice alongside the bottled lemon juice in most grocery stores. You can substitute lemon juice, but the flavor won't be as tart.

½ (14-ounce) can fat-free sweetened condensed milk (about ½ cup)
¼ cup Key lime juice
¾ cup plus 2 tablespoons frozen fat-free whipped topping, thawed and divided
6 (3-inch) graham cracker tart shells
12 strawberries, sliced

1. Combine condensed milk, lime juice, and ½ cup whipped topping, stirring with a whisk.

2. Pour filling evenly into tart shells. Cover and chill 30 minutes or until ready to serve. Top tarts evenly with strawberries and remaining ¼ cup whipped topping. Yield: 6 servings (serving size: 1 tart, 2 tablespoons strawberry slices, and about 1 tablespoon whipped topping).

prep: 2 minutes ∞ **cook:** 8 minutes

Caramelized Peaches with Vanilla Frozen Yogurt

pictured on page 119

You can use apricots instead of peaches if you wish, or try a combination of both. Apricots are smaller than peaches, so plan on two apricots per serving.

- 1/4 cup packed brown sugar
- 1/4 teaspoon ground cinnamon
- Cooking spray
- 4 large peaches, halved and pitted
- 1/2 cup plus 2 teaspoons water, divided
- 2 cups vanilla fat-free frozen yogurt

1. Combine brown sugar and cinnamon, and set aside.

2. Heat a large nonstick skillet over medium-high heat; coat pan with cooking spray. Add peaches; cook 3 minutes on each side. While peaches cook, add 1/2 cup water to pan, 1 tablespoon at a time, and cook until liquid evaporates. Remove fruit.

3. Add brown sugar mixture and 2 teaspoons water to pan; cook 2 minutes or until syrupy.

4. Divide frozen yogurt evenly among 4 bowls. Top with peaches and sugar syrup. Yield: 4 servings (serving size: 1/2 cup frozen yogurt, 2 peach halves, and 1/2 tablespoon syrup).

***POINTS* value: 4**

per serving:
CALORIES 214
FAT 0.4g (saturated fat 0g)
PROTEIN 5.4g
CARBOHYDRATE 49.5g
FIBER 2.4g
CHOLESTEROL 0mg
IRON 1.2mg
SODIUM 85mg
CALCIUM 122mg

TIP: If your peaches are firm, let them stand on the kitchen counter for a few days until they're soft to the touch.

prep: 9 minutes ∞ **cook:** 10 minutes

Peach Shortcakes

Turbinado sugar, with its unique texture and amber color, gives these shortcakes a sweet crunch as well as an elegant appearance.

***POINTS* value: 5**

per serving:
CALORIES 250
FAT 5.2g (saturated fat 1.9g)
PROTEIN 4g
CARBOHYDRATE 46.9g
FIBER 1.2g
CHOLESTEROL 8mg
IRON 1.5mg
SODIUM 399mg
CALCIUM 155mg

TIP: Use a fork to quickly toss together the ingredients for the dough. Over-mixing will cause the shortcake to be tough.

- 1 cup plus 2 tablespoons low-fat baking mix (such as Bisquick Heart Smart)
- 3 tablespoons granulated sugar, divided
- ⅛ teaspoon ground cinnamon
- ⅛ teaspoon ground nutmeg
- ⅓ cup 1% low-fat milk
- 1 tablespoon butter, melted
- 2 teaspoons turbinado sugar
- 3 cups frozen sliced peaches
- ¼ cup frozen fat-free whipped topping, thawed

1. Preheat oven to 425°.

2. Lightly spoon 1 cup baking mix into a dry measuring cup; level with a knife. Combine 1 cup plus 2 tablespoons baking mix with next 3 ingredients; stir well. Add milk and butter, stirring just until combined.

3. Form dough into 4 (3-inch) circles on an ungreased baking sheet. Sprinkle each with ½ teaspoon turbinado sugar. Bake at 425° for 10 minutes or until lightly golden.

4. While shortcakes bake, sprinkle peaches with remaining 1 tablespoon granulated sugar; stir well. Microwave at HIGH 3 minutes.

5. Split each shortcake in half horizontally. Place bottom halves of cakes on dessert plates. Top each with ¾ cup peach mixture and 1 tablespoon whipped topping. Top with remaining cake halves. Serve warm. Yield: 4 servings (serving size: 1 shortcake).

prep: 2 minutes ∞ **other:** 2 hours

Piña Colada Granita

This frozen dessert doesn't require an ice-cream maker—just freeze the mixture in a pan and scrape with a fork. Serve this dessert to cool the heat from a spicy meal or the summer sun.

2 (6-ounce) cans pineapple juice
1 (11.8-ounce) can coconut water
1 tablespoon fresh lime juice
1/8 teaspoon rum flavoring

1. Stir together all ingredients; pour into a 13 x 9–inch baking dish. Cover and freeze 2 hours, scraping with a fork every 30 minutes. Remove mixture from freezer; scrape entire mixture with a fork until fluffy. Serve immediately, or spoon into a freezer-safe container; cover and freeze up to 1 month. Yield: 6 servings (serving size: 1/2 cup).

***POINTS* value: 1**

per serving:
CALORIES 56
FAT 0.2g (saturated fat 0g)
PROTEIN 0.2g
CARBOHYDRATE 13.8g
FIBER 0.3g
CHOLESTEROL 0mg
IRON 0.3mg
SODIUM 22mg
CALCIUM 23mg

TIP: Coconut water and coconut milk are different products. You can find both in the Mexican or Latin section of your supermarket, so read the labels carefully to make sure you purchase the correct one.

prep: 10 minutes

Pumpkin Mousse Parfaits

The flavors of this simple weeknight dessert will remind you of traditional pumpkin pie. These parfaits are the perfect ending to a savory dinner of Peach-Glazed Pork Tenderloin (page 67) and steamed green beans.

***POINTS* value: 5**

per serving:
CALORIES 234
FAT 5.8g (saturated fat 3.1g)
PROTEIN 3.6g
CARBOHYDRATE 34.7g
FIBER 1.8g
CHOLESTEROL 14mg
IRON 1.2mg
SODIUM 284mg
CALCIUM 24mg

TIP: To make gingersnap crumbs, place the cookies in a heavy-duty zip-top bag, and crush them with a rolling pin.

1½ cups canned pumpkin pie filling
½ cup (4 ounces) block-style ⅓-less-fat cream cheese
3 cups frozen fat-free whipped topping, thawed and divided
¾ cup gingersnap crumbs (about 12 cookies, finely crushed)

1. Combine pie filling and cream cheese in a large bowl; beat with a mixer at medium speed until smooth. Fold in 1½ cups whipped topping.

2. Spoon 1 tablespoon gingersnap crumbs into each of 6 parfait glasses; top each with about ¼ cup pumpkin mixture and 2 tablespoons whipped topping. Repeat layers once. Serve immediately, or cover and chill until ready to serve. Yield: 6 servings (serving size: 1 parfait).

prep: 5 minutes

Chocolate-Strawberry Malts

Serve this dessert beverage with Roast Beef Wraps (page 17) for a meal with a *POINTS* value of 8. The malts melt quickly, so prepare them at the end of the meal and serve immediately along with a straw, if desired.

1¼ cups frozen unsweetened whole strawberries
¾ cup 1% low-fat milk
3 tablespoons malted milk powder
2 tablespoons chocolate syrup
2 cups chocolate light ice cream

1. Place first 4 ingredients in a blender, and process until smooth. Add ice cream, and process until blended. Yield: 4 servings (serving size: about ¾ cup).

***POINTS* value: 4**

per serving:
CALORIES 193
FAT 4.5g (saturated fat 2.6g)
PROTEIN 5.5g
CARBOHYDRATE 32.1g
FIBER 2g
CHOLESTEROL 23mg
IRON 0.5mg
SODIUM 100mg
CALCIUM 134mg

TIP: Find malted milk powder on your grocer's shelves near the other powdered and canned milk products. Chocolate malted milk powder is available, too.

prep: 5 minutes ∞ **cook:** 42 minutes ∞ **other:** 3 hours

Chocolate-Coconut Mousse

This silky-smooth dessert is reminiscent of the flavors in a popular chocolate and coconut candy bar. Sprinkle the mousse with toasted sliced almonds before serving, if desired.

***POINTS* value: 6**

per serving:
CALORIES 246
FAT 12.8g (saturated fat 6.7g)
PROTEIN 5.5g
CARBOHYDRATE 25.3g
FIBER 0.1g
CHOLESTEROL 0mg
IRON 0.9mg
SODIUM 85mg
CALCIUM 26mg

TIP: Tofu varies in texture—from creamy and smooth to firm enough to slice. For this recipe, use silken or Japanese-style soft tofu that has a delicate, custardlike texture.

- ½ cup light coconut milk
- ½ cup dark chocolate chips
- 12 ounces silken-style soft tofu, drained
- 2 tablespoons cornstarch
- 2 teaspoons coconut extract
- ⅛ teaspoon salt
- Frozen reduced-calorie whipped topping, thawed (optional)

1. Preheat oven to 325°.

2. Combine coconut milk and chocolate chips in a small saucepan. Cook over medium-high heat 2 to 3 minutes or just until chocolate melts, stirring constantly.

3. Place tofu and next 3 ingredients in a food processor or blender; process until well blended. Add chocolate mixture; process until smooth. Spoon into 4 (4-ounce) ramekins; place ramekins in an 8-inch baking pan. Add water to pan to a depth of 1 inch.

4. Cover pan with foil, and bake at 325° for 40 minutes or until set. Remove from oven; place plastic wrap directly on surface of mousse. Let cool completely on a wire rack (about 1 hour). Chill at least 2 hours. Serve with whipped topping, if desired. Yield: 4 servings (serving size: 1 mousse).

prep: 18 minutes ∞ **other:** 30 minutes

Chocolate-Raspberry Charlottes

These beautiful individually molded desserts feature raspberry-soaked ladyfingers that surround chocolate pudding. With a quick prep time and an elegant appearance, these desserts are ideal when you have weeknight dinner guests.

12 cakelike ladyfingers, split horizontally and halved
⅓ cup seedless raspberry jam, melted
1 (2.1-ounce) package sugar-free chocolate instant pudding mix
2 cups fat-free milk
¾ cup frozen reduced-calorie whipped topping, thawed
Fresh raspberries (optional)

1. Line 6 (6-ounce) custard cups with plastic wrap. Line bottom and sides of each dish with 8 ladyfinger pieces (cut sides facing inward). Brush ladyfingers with melted raspberry jam.

2. Prepare chocolate pudding according to package directions using 2 cups fat-free milk. Spoon ⅓ cup pudding into each custard cup. Cover and chill at least 30 minutes. Invert cups onto dessert plates. Remove plastic wrap. Top each serving with 2 tablespoons whipped topping. Garnish with fresh raspberries, if desired. Yield: 6 servings (serving size: 1 charlotte).

***POINTS* value: 4**

per serving:
CALORIES 178
FAT 2g (saturated fat 1.3g)
PROTEIN 5.5g
CARBOHYDRATE 35.2g
FIBER 1.1g
CHOLESTEROL 31mg
IRON 0.2mg
SODIUM 421mg
CALCIUM 123mg

TIP: Look for ladyfingers in the bakery or the frozen-food section of the supermarket. We used soft ladyfingers, which are made to be split.

prep: 9 minutes ∞ **cook:** 18 minutes ∞ **other:** 3 hours and 10 minutes

Chocolate Cream Pie

pictured on page 47

Treat yourself with this luscious pie! It received our Test Kitchens' highest rating, so it's definitely worth spending some of your weekly *POINTS* Allowance.

***POINTS* value: 6**

per serving:
CALORIES 271
FAT 10.9g (saturated fat 6.3g)
PROTEIN 4.9g
CARBOHYDRATE 38.7g
FIBER 0.7g
CHOLESTEROL 7mg
IRON 0.6mg
SODIUM 223mg
CALCIUM 97mg

TIP: Before unfolding, let refrigerated crust stand at room temperature for 15 to 20 minutes, or microwave one pouch on Defrost (30% power) for 20 to 40 seconds.

½ (15-ounce) package refrigerated pie dough (such as Pillsbury)
2 cups fat-free milk
1 teaspoon unflavored gelatin
1 (5-ounce) package chocolate cook-and-serve pudding mix
¼ cup dark chocolate chips (such as Hershey's)
1 (8-ounce) container frozen reduced-calorie whipped topping, thawed
Cocoa powder (optional)

1. Preheat oven to 450°.

2. Fit pie dough in a 9-inch pie plate. Fold edges under, and flute. Pierce bottom and sides of dough with a fork.

3. Bake at 450° for 10 minutes or until lightly browned.

4. While crust cools, combine milk and gelatin in a medium saucepan; let stand 5 minutes. Add pudding mix, stirring with a whisk until blended. Cook over medium heat 8 minutes or until pudding mixture comes to a boil, stirring constantly with whisk. Remove from heat, and add chocolate chips, stirring until melted. Place pan in an ice-water bath about 5 minutes or until cool, stirring pudding mixture often.

5. Pour filling into piecrust. Cover surface of filling with plastic wrap. Refrigerate 3 hours or until thoroughly chilled.

6. Spread whipped topping over pie before serving. Sprinkle with cocoa powder, if desired. Yield: 8 servings (serving size: 1 slice).

prep: 10 minutes ∞ **cook:** 19 minutes

Chocolate Sponge Cake Cupcakes

Dutch process cocoa gives these cupcakes a rich brown color.

Cooking spray
1 cup all-purpose flour
3 tablespoons Dutch process cocoa (such as Hershey's Special Dark)
1 teaspoon baking powder
¼ teaspoon salt
½ cup 1% low-fat milk
2 tablespoons light stick butter
2 large eggs
1 cup sugar
2 teaspoons vanilla extract
1½ cups frozen fat-free whipped topping, thawed

1. Preheat oven to 350°.

2. Place 12 paper muffin cup liners in muffin cups; coat liners with cooking spray. Set aside.

3. Lightly spoon flour into a dry measuring cup; level with a knife. Sift together flour and next 3 ingredients.

4. Combine milk and butter in a 1-cup glass measure, and microwave at HIGH 1 to 1½ minutes or until butter melts.

5. Beat eggs and sugar with a mixer at high speed 5 minutes. Add flour mixture, milk mixture, and vanilla. Beat at medium speed 30 seconds or until smooth. Spoon batter into prepared muffin cups.

6. Bake at 350° for 18 minutes or until cupcakes spring back when touched lightly in center. Cool cupcakes in pan on a wire rack 10 minutes; remove from pan, and cool completely. Spoon 2 tablespoons whipped topping onto each cupcake just before serving. Yield: 12 cupcakes (serving size: 1 cupcake).

***POINTS* value: 3**

per serving:
CALORIES 150
FAT 3.3g (saturated fat 0.9g)
PROTEIN 2.7g
CARBOHYDRATE 28.3g
FIBER 0.5g
CHOLESTEROL 38mg
IRON 1.1mg
SODIUM 127mg
CALCIUM 41mg

TIP: If desired, you can substitute natural or nonalkalized cocoa for the Dutch process (alkalized) cocoa, but you won't get the same dark brown color, and there will be a subtle flavor difference.

prep: 6 minutes ∞ **cook:** 23 minutes ∞ **other:** 10 minutes

Raisin Brownie Bars

pictured on page 113

If you're craving chocolate, these dark and fudgy brownie bars are sure to satisfy. The mixture is very thick and requires a standing time of 10 minutes to allow the dry ingredients to moisten, but the wait is definitely worth it!

***POINTS* value: 3**

per serving:
CALORIES 123
FAT 3.7g (saturated fat 2.1g)
PROTEIN 1.9g
CARBOHYDRATE 22.1g
FIBER 0.8g
CHOLESTEROL 19mg
IRON 0.5mg
SODIUM 38mg
CALCIUM 17mg

TIP: For a dark chocolate variation, substitute dark chocolate–covered raisins for the milk-chocolate version.

- ⅔ cup all-purpose flour
- 1 cup sugar
- ½ cup unsweetened cocoa
- ½ teaspoon baking powder
- 3 tablespoons butter, melted
- 1 large egg
- 1 large egg white
- ½ cup milk chocolate–covered raisins (such as Nestlé Raisinets)
- Cooking spray

1. Preheat oven to 350°.

2. Lightly spoon flour into dry measuring cups; level with a knife. Combine flour and next 6 ingredients in a medium bowl, stirring well until dry ingredients are moistened (mixture will be thick). Let mixture stand 10 minutes. Fold in chocolate-covered raisins.

3. Press mixture into an 8-inch square pan coated with cooking spray. Bake at 350° for 23 to 25 minutes. Cool in pan on a wire rack. Yield: 16 servings (serving size: 1 bar).

Index

10 Simple Core Plan® Side Dishes

Vegetable	Servings	Preparation	Cooking Instructions
Asparagus	3 to 4 per pound	Snap off tough ends. Remove scales, if desired.	To steam: Cook, covered, on a rack above boiling water 2 to 3 minutes. To boil: Cook, covered, in a small amount of boiling water 2 to 3 minutes or until crisp-tender.
Broccoli	3 to 4 per pound	Remove outer leaves and tough ends of lower stalks. Wash; cut into spears.	To steam: Cook, covered, on a rack above boiling water 5 to 7 minutes or until crisp-tender.
Carrots	4 per pound	Scrape; remove ends, and rinse. Leave tiny carrots whole; slice large carrots.	To steam: Cook, covered, on a rack above boiling water 8 to 10 minutes or until crisp-tender. To boil: Cook, covered, in a small amount of boiling water 8 to 10 minutes or until crisp-tender.
Cauliflower	4 per medium head	Remove outer leaves and stalk. Wash. Break into florets.	To steam: Cook, covered, on a rack above boiling water 5 to 7 minutes or until crisp-tender.
Corn	4 per 4 large ears	Remove husks and silks. Leave corn on the cob, or cut off kernels.	Cook, covered, in boiling water to cover 8 to 10 minutes (on cob) or in a small amount of boiling water 4 to 6 minutes (kernels).
Green beans	4 per pound	Wash; trim ends, and remove strings. Cut into 1½-inch pieces.	To steam: Cook, covered, on a rack above boiling water 5 to 7 minutes. To boil: Cook, covered, in a small amount of boiling water 5 to 7 minutes or until crisp-tender.
Potatoes	3 to 4 per pound	Scrub; peel, if desired. Leave whole, slice, or cut into chunks.	To boil: Cook, covered, in boiling water to cover 30 to 40 minutes (whole) or 15 to 20 minutes (slices or chunks). To bake: Bake at 400° for 1 hour or until done.
Snow peas	4 per pound	Wash; trim ends, and remove tough strings.	To steam: Cook, covered, on a rack above boiling water 2 to 3 minutes. Or sauté in cooking spray or 1 teaspoon oil over medium-high heat 3 to 4 minutes or until crisp-tender.
Squash, summer	3 to 4 per pound	Wash; trim ends, and slice or chop.	To steam: Cook, covered, on a rack above boiling water 6 to 8 minutes.To boil: Cook, covered, in a small amount of boiling water 6 to 8 minutes or until crisp-tender.
Squash, winter (including acorn, butternut, and buttercup)	2 per pound	Rinse; cut in half, and remove all seeds. Leave in halves to bake, or peel and cube to boil.	To boil: Cook cubes, covered, in boiling water 20 to 25 minutes. To bake: Place halves, cut sides down, in a shallow baking dish; add ½ inch water. Bake, uncovered, at 375° for 30 minutes. Turn and season, or fill; bake an additional 20 to 30 minutes or until tender.